Confessions
from
Left Field

Confessions from Left Field

A Baseball Pilgrimage

RAYMOND MUNGO

E. P. DUTTON, INC.   New York

For my parents

Copyright © 1983 by Raymond Mungo

Published in the United States by E. P. Dutton, Inc.,
2 Park Avenue, New York, N.Y. 10016

Library of Congress Cataloging in Publication Data

Mungo, Raymond
    Confessions from left field.
    1. Baseball. !. Title.
GV867.3.M86   1983   796.357   82-18322

ISBN: 0-525-24168-X

Published simultaneously in Canada by Clarke, Irwin & Company
Limited, Toronto and Vancouver

10 9 8 7 6 5 4 3 2 1

First Edition

The poem by Richard Coutant on page 73 is copyright © 1983 by
Richard Coutant and is reprinted by permission of the author.

Contents

Preface

Baseball is a game that is 90 percent mental; and the other half is physical.
                                                              —Yogi Berra

You have to be careful what you dream because so often dreams come true. Anyway, who's to say we don't live in our dreams as real-ly as we do in waking reality?

My particular dream is in direct opposition to my personal nightmare. I strive to escape my natural fears and worries about the direction this world is taking; to avoid having to consider Ronald Reagan as more than a cowboy in the movies of my childhood; to soothe the anxieties of depression, radiation, the draft, the sure feeling in my stomach that it's time to get hot, to get involved, lest we all be blown to pieces.

But involvement on a political level usually leads to confrontations with authority, which leads to a life of constant stress. Where are we supposed to turn for personal peace of mind in a world like this?

I found a relief valve at the ball park.

Not any particular ball park, but the park itself, the green field, the diamond, is my shining shrine. Oh, you can go out to the ballgame and spend your time worrying about your late mortgage payment or the situation abroad in whatever trouble spot the media is featuring that week or anything else that's poisoning your mind. But the general idea is to swill a lot of beer and get a suntan on your belly button and yell your head off. Let off steam. Relax. There is no clock and the game is theoretically endless, as are the towering columns of statistics and panoply of strategies. I lose myself in the scholarship of ball.

If the game is a good one, even if no pennant or world championship is on the line, it is one of the things in life that has the power to distract me from serious considerations. Consider the value of *that*. If you take the world at face value, you'll go crazy, and good psychiatrists are very expensive. Baseball is one of the cheapest obsessions you could have. It's virtually free on the airwaves (although excessive exposure to bad oil-company and beer ads may have long-range carcinogenic effects), and you can still buy a ticket to any ball park in the major leagues for less than the price of a movie. However, baseball can be a jealous witch.

I had a good life, living in California, a life full of sunshine, friends, flowers, white wine, in an environment that promoted eccentricity. I had stumbled luckily onto an island of stability, a community of exceptional friends, amid the loose sands of the central coast. Coastal Californians are spoiled by good weather and easy access to party supplies, so that many become constitutionally incapable of surviving in rougher climes—which is just about everywhere. I felt this dreaded virus growing in my own body, like a softening of the bones. I was in great jeopardy of becoming a Californian, who'd sink when the inevitable quakes came. On balmy December days, I enjoyed reading of the blizzards back East. I had not set foot in winter for ten years, but it seemed time to toughen up.

To get going, I had to break free of a situation many writers idealize: a perfect picture-window cabin overlooking the Big Sur coastline, with kind and acutely sensitive neighbors whose hospitality is warm, whose liquor cabinets are full. From my perch in the center of the state, I monitored all five baseball teams in California on radio and TV and threw my emotional support to the San Francisco Giants, who are as lost a cause as my previous heart throbs, the Seattle Mariners, but in a more insidious way. You *know* the Mariners are going to lose, but the Giants string you along. At the peak of my Giants fanhood, I went to the fanciest Carmel parties wearing radio headphones tuned to the Giants game, prescription sunglasses, and various Giants regalia. The one thing the Giants had going for them was that they were better than the Oakland A's across the bay. Which was not saying much.

I was awarded a fellowship in baseball studies at the prestigious Carmel Institute, which provided everything necessary to creative work, including the cabin and IBM Selectric. I paid what rent I could retroactively, every time I got a royalty check, and made a subsistence living as the neighborhood babysitter.

My fellowship at the institute enabled me to devote myself to baseball studies full-time for two years—time spent deep in the record and rules books, in the rich literature of the game from Ring Lardner's *You Know Me Al* to Roger Angell's *Five Seasons*, and in the exotic language of statistics. I told myself this was training toward eventually becoming an Official Scorer. But my passion for the game is epic, and I follow it of free inclination.

You stay in paradise only as long as you can see the trees; you wake up some morning in December, just before Christmas, say, and you don't notice the sunshine, hear the birds, or see the sea. You're a burned-out brother. It's hard to tear yourself away, especially for a place like Phoenix, Arizona, where the spring training camps open in March. Your real nut can't wait for the season to open.

ONE

The Last Great Season

1

Baseball has the advantage over cricket of being sooner ended.
                              —George Bernard Shaw

Many people say baseball is boring, and they're right. That's what's great about it. A spectacular play stands out vividly, an individual achievement, after minutes or hours of nothing-happening. Baseball is the only game in which the Perfect Game is one in which nothing happens at all—no hits, runs, walks, errors, no men on base. (I met an eighty-year-old man who had seen only one major league game in his life, Don Larsen's perfect game in the 1956 World Series. "Nothing happened," he complained, "but everybody went crazy.")

Life is boring in the same sense. The occasional great event is the spice of living, but most of it consists of breathing and eating and eliminating—and working. You're lucky indeed if your work inspires you to the point that you enthuse about it in your "free" time. Baseball offers that familiar routine day in and out. . . . "A bouncing ball toward short . . . Mendoza gloves it in midair . . . and throws to first for the out. And the side is retired." Whew. Yawn.

3

"Making out" is very good in high school, but bad in baseball. Even the best hitter makes an out two out of three times at bat. Ted Williams was the last player to hit .400 or more, and that was forty years ago, although George Brett came close at .390 in 1980. Three-ninety is spectacular, but it ain't .400. Baseball is precise.

Some people think Shakespeare is boring, too. Boredom is probably the single greatest cause of death in this country. In Japanese baseball, it's exactly the opposite: overexertion is the big killer. The fans organize themselves into maniacal cheering sections, and cheer and clap in unison under the direction of flag-waving leaders. They are permitted to lose their minds in unison after a home run or other great feat. And the game is permitted to end in a *tie*—an incomprehensible violation of baseball morality.

Remember, if you can, that spring of 1980. The tables had been turned. We puzzled why, *why* did Jimmy Carter let the shah of Iran into New York for surgery that might as well have been performed elsewhere? The attendant seizure of the embassy in Iran and holding of United States bureaucrats as hostages gave the American people a focus for hatred and aggression they hadn't had since the last war. The apparent evil was nicely personified in a fanatical ayatollah, while only the most sophisticated people bothered to note that the ex-shah had been something of a rotter himself.

All of that had nothing to do with baseball, but everything to do with the climate in which baseball roused itself to the new season in this, the Decade of Anxiety. Running off to spring training in Arizona that March was tantamount to ducking responsibility. While the world burned, grown men engaged in ritualistic play—epic drinking, massive exposure to sunshine after the gloom of February, sitting around swimming pools, eating steaks, driving air-conditioned Plymouths, and of course playing a little ball. Who could resist?

When I stepped into Amtrak's Coast Starlight on the first leg of my journey between northern California and Phoenix, all sense of home departed from my heart and I laughed maniacally at the neatness of the Escape. People were going to *work* every morning, grumpy from the news in the morning paper; to their offices, factories, and farms; while I was going to sit in the sun and watch boys play ball. And the only way to get there, of course, was on a traveling party with company, drinks, joints, scenery, food, and who knows what? The ultimate in Amtrak Euphoria is the private Econo-Roomette with flask of cognac and a tiny vial of nasal remedies. But on this particular trip, I was light on cash and limited to the club car and coaches.

Passengers on long-distance Amtrak trains have a lot of time to kill, so unless you're made of stone you'll wind up having long conversations with strangers you'd never otherwise meet. A grandmother sitting next to me in the bar told me her life story; her eight-year-old grandson, who appeared periodically while running up and down the train, had been left on her doorstep, literally, by her no-good daughter who'd gone off and married an Indian out in the pueblo. The daughter had never been seen again. Grandma Betty and the kid lived in Phoenix, Santa Fe, and Taos. The kid went to school, sort of, in various places. Betty ordered another gin and tonic, and bought one for me. They'd run up to Fresno to see her sister-in-law and look for work, but when nothing

5

panned out she decided to head back to Phoenix, where she could always get work as a housekeeper. Desert people are not like you and me. It takes some internal fortitude to survive all the nothing. Plant scientists and the like would point out that the desert is teeming with life, but for most people desert life is measured in casinos, shopping malls, and neighborhoods. Betty bought two more drinks. The train hit the endlessly blue coast at Santa Barbara. Sunset: good-bye to my Lord.

Pleasantly smashed, we floated into Los Angeles. Union Station in downtown L.A. is the most painless access to the metropolis; statuesque, grand old train station of my dreams! I had a few hours to kill before the eastbound train was to leave, and called an old friend who'd arrived in town as a novelist and screenwriter and had evolved into a real estate agent. When our crowd was young, Bill spent all his time in Moroccan jellabas getting stoned, chanting, meditating, burning incense. Now he won't touch a joint until his day's and night's frenetic dealings are closed. Superficial newspaper features point to someone like Bill and say, "There went the generation that wanted revolution." I prefer to think it's just another stage in Bill's evolution.

2

Anyone who wants to understand the heart and mind of America had better study baseball.
—Jacques Barzun

I landed in Phoenix high on the mistaken assumption that one could simply take a bus to the ball park. It took a while of questioning to find out that there's absolutely no public transportation to any of the stadia. In short, you need a car or a pair of strong legs. I did catch a Greyhound from downtown Phoenix to Sun City, where the Milwaukee Brewers were hosting the Seattle Mariners in an exhibition game. The driver let me out a mile from the park but there were no sidewalks so I had to walk under the blazing sun on the shoulder of a four-lane highway. Sun City is a retirement community where, I was told, you must be at least fifty-five years old to buy a house. The local men's Lions Club sold beer and hot dogs at fair prices and it cost two dollars to enter, for which you can sit close enough to touch the players. The afternoon passed in a mental fog.

I called some friends who graciously came out to pick me up. Michael and Susan lived in Phoenix so that she could finish her nursing education, but they were native

Californians who hated the place. The town has a mean edge for sure. Every day's newspaper featured murders that nobody would be prosecuted for. A landlady shot her tenant in an argument over back rent; she's pictured in the news casually pointing out the spot where she killed him to the police officer taking the report. A guy in a bar made obscene remarks about another guy's mother, so the second fellow shot the first. Who could blame him? Not the Phoenix prosecutor.

This is the wild West, too wild for me. Gunshops line the downtown streets. A certain white Republican song is in the air. These are the people of Phoenix: old people, retirees living on pensions, driving around in air-conditioned American cars with the windows up and doors locked; Indian and Hispanic peoples in brightly colored clothes; *mamacitas*, old winos; "white trash" people who fight in bars. I ducked out of the heat in a place called Poor Richard's and asked for a Stolichnaya over ice: "Honey, we don't got none of that Russian vodka, check out the name of this place." The ball parks are havens of sunny delight but when the final out is made and the sun mercifully quits, the entertainment is limited to the restaurant circuit.

You can golf in Phoenix if you can stand the heat. And you can get a haircut for two dollars; the sign in the barber shop reads "We don't have styles. Regular. Or Short." (I had the regular and believe me, it was short.)

Spring training is an annual exercise in sloth for the fans and writers, and even the players don't seem to go through any particularly grueling ordeals. (The Japanese teams who now share camps in Arizona with our major teams are the exception. They get up at dawn and run and stretch and work like demons till the sun goes

8

down. One of these Nipponese sluggers, a certain Yakult Swallow, wrote a poem called "Living Hell in the Batting Cage at Yuma.") There's a lot of drinking and eating out and hanging around Ramada Inns. I'd have my first beer at noon, while watching the batting practice, and my first serious drink of the day around four, when the game was over. Game time was spent in another space: baseball time stands still.

The games themselves are of no importance. They don't "count." The idea is to give all the players a chance to warm up for the season or prove themselves, and not even Pete Rose gets in a whole game. From a fan's point of view, these games can be disappointing. When you're trailing by a run in the seventh and your best hitter is due up, he's suddenly replaced by a pinch-hitter you never heard of, who promptly strikes out.

Still, from a purist's view the whole process of evolution is fascinating to watch. Younger players come to spring training in hopes of catching the eye of a scout, manager, or coach and making a big league roster. Every spring has its young phenoms, and it's fun to watch them progress. Somewhere down the line, when the player is a star, you can say you saw him as a nineteen-year-old hopeful out of Wichita or Salt Lake City. The experience can be disheartening for these lads. Most will be "cut" and shipped back to the minors when the real season opens and the teams are forced to limit themselves to twenty-five players.

Consider the plight of the Albuquerque Dukes, the Dodgers' Triple-A farm club. It's so loaded with talent that it dominates the Pacific Coast League every year, destroying any suspense in the PCL pennant race. Many of the Dukes are of major league caliber right now, but they can't crack the Dodgers' exceptionally established lineup and are forced to toil in the bushes, endure long bus rides, stay in cheap motels, and live on low wages. If the Dodgers ever let Steve Garvey go, which it appears they might, watch for young Mike Marshall or Greg Brock to rise from Albuquerque to overnight glory in L.A.

I remember a promising Seattle outfielder named Rodney Craig, with whom I shared happy beers on the night after he hit a home run in an exhibition game. A very dignified, soft-spoken, twenty-one-year-old giant, he was high on life that night, but was shipped down to Spokane the next day. Nothing's worse than Spokane once you've had the fine wine of the big circuit. What do you say to a kid who's being sent down despite having "it," having the ability to make it in the big leagues? You say, "Don't worry, kid, you'll be back." That got a smile from shy Rodney Craig. (And he *will* be back, too. You read it here first.*)

Aside from players on their way up, spring training always features those on their way down. There's nothing sadder than seeing one of your old favorite heroes, Detroit's great slugger Willie Horton, for example, unable to cut the mustard anymore and sent down to Portland. To jump ahead a few springs, Gaylord Perry in 1982 could find only one club, the Mariners, willing to give him a tryout. It looked like the end for ancient Gaylord, self-confessed spitball artist, three victories shy of the magic 300 mark. But Seattle took the old gent on, and of course he won his three hundredth game and then some. (It's a comment on the anemic attendance in Seattle that fewer than 28,000 fans showed up to see

*N.B. Craig *is* back, picked up by the Cleveland Indians in late '82.

Perry's three hundredth win, but 36,000 showed a few days later to get free "funny nose glasses.")

Rumors fly in spring training camps faster than anywhere else except Hollywood. Have you seen that kid, Steve Balboni, that the Yanks have? Kid can crush 'em. Word is out that Steinbrenner will part with so-and-so to get Garvey. Players are quick to notice when the opposing catcher has a weak arm. Poor Milt May, catching for the Giants, was dubbed "Venus de Milo" by the press corps. No arm. May recovered; some don't. The writers and fans sit around bullshitting about all the latest gossip, and the players are as close and accessible as they'll ever be. Some of the ball parks have nothing more than flimsy fences separating players from fans, and it's easy to shake your hero's hand.

"Hey, Billy, how ya doin'? Gonna get in the game today?"

"Yeah, just *about*. They'll only give me three innings. Sheeet." (Billy North, Giants' outfielder 1978–79.)

"Hey, Vida! You pitchin' today?"

"Where you been, girl? I pitched against Cleveland yesterday. What newspaper do you read?" (Vida Blue, pitcher.)

"*The Sacramento Bee.*"

"You from Sacramento?"

"Yeah."

"You really *have* been somewhere else."

There is a delicious elixir of nonsense about such banter, and a great and powerful joy at seeing the boys back on the field and knowing that the game is with us again, after the barren winter.

The only danger in the easy interaction between fans and players is that you may see some of your heroes a little too closely. They may seem like human beings,

11

rather oversize ones, and not really as magical and wonderful as you thought. Reggie Jackson was quoted by the New York *Daily News* as screaming "I hate kids!" while turning away a tearful eight-year-old who asked for his autograph. There's nothing especially romantic about a planeload of drunken players insulting the stewardesses with sexist jokes. Some of these guys are yahoos, just older versions of the crude jocks you knew in high school or college.

But certain old favorites will always be great human beings and great baseball stars, even past their primes, in our memory.

I kept book on my favorites, like Willie McCovey ("Number 44" was driving his Lincoln with license tag WM 44 when I caught him at a stop sign in the Phoenix Municipal Stadium parking lot), and trudged home nightly to my bottle and sleeping mat. Phoenix TV went off the air at midnight. Sultry winds, blasts of humid heat, kept the nights heavy and oppressive.

Every year I go to Arizona planning to spend three weeks, and leave after a week grateful to escape alive. My natural attraction to the game is balanced by my loathing for the city of Phoenix, and I can't take it anymore. I may have to lay off the Cactus League until I can afford all the amenities.

3

Dream into the open spaces of the baseball turf,
even if you're not there at the park. You're there
anyway.
  —Marvin Cohen, in *Baseball the Beautiful*

I retreated from Phoenix back to California only to
leave in time to open the 1980 season in Boston. Took the
Empire Builder Amtrak train from Seattle to New York
with the Econo-Roomette and all of Montana at my feet.
Changed to the Broadway Limited in Chicago, where
the East in all its antiquity and congestion starts to fill
open spaces with houses, buildings, people, and dogs,
and the standards of inside scenery come crashing down.
Amtrak operates its new Superliners only west of Chicago. The eastern third of the nation also has older
tracks, more congested routes, more breakdowns and
delays. Outside the populace trudges toward work and
payments on their insurance policies, cursing weather,
taxes, and the ayatollah.
  Coming home to Boston after mixing blood with California always throws me into a kind of paranoid nostal-
gia. I am as sentimental as any West Coast New England-
er about old monuments, parks, museums, and

13

landmarks of Boston. At the same time, a dark fear
comes over me, a fear of winter and hardship and
aggravation, of dying in Boston. Boston takes the Red
Sox seriously.

4

I dreamed Ted Williams leaning at night against
the Eiffel Tower, weeping.
                                        —Gregory Corso,
                        from "Dream of a Baseball Star"

I must have been about ten years old when Jimmy
Piersall, Red Sox outfielder, came to my hometown of
Lawrence, Massachusetts, to pitch Cain's potato chips
and sign autographs for the kiddies. As I recall, you
actually had to buy a bag of chips to get access to
Piersall, who later became chiefly famous for losing his
mind on the field, attacking the fans and then retreating
into what in those days we called "the nuthouse"; then
coming back to the Red Sox and authoring his movie/
autobiography *Fear Strikes Out*. Piersall now works for
the Chicago White Sox as a broadcaster/*enfant terrible*,
and is still involved in fisticuffs and off-the-cuffs that
drive the management crazy. He's a likable lout, a kind
of baseball saint who takes the game *seriously*, who just
plain hates to lose. Billy Martin's from the same mold,
and although people complain that these brawling drink-
ers put baseball in a poor light, they are the actual
heroes of the masses. They are real guys who get pissed

off. Then, watch out! The fans love a bench-clearing melee on the diamond, even if they deplore the bad sportsmanship.

I was awestruck as Jimmy Piersall's big meaty hand squeezed the life out of my own puny one. I resolved to play baseball, even if I was the smallest kid in class and spent all my spare time reading books. I went to Little League tryouts one Saturday morning with my kid brother, who must have been seven. On my first time at bat, I hit a long fly ball to right field that sailed over the fielder's head, bounced once, and went over a fence into an old lady's backyard. No way of retrieving that ball!

I stood at the plate watching the ball and not moving. "Run home! Run home!" I could hear my little brother's voice and the voices of the others. So I turned and ran—home, to my house, to my books. End of career. My kid brother, of course, made the team.

The next time I made an appearance on the diamond was in the 1980 softball season at Newburyport, Massachusetts, when I was shanghaied by that same kid brother into pitching for the industrial league he managed. Only eight players had shown up and Michael, of Michael's Harborside Restaurant and Bar—where the team hangs out before and after the games—was not happy about losing out to the finest lineups the other saloons in town could offer just because my brother had lost his pitcher.

On the night I was chosen we were pitted against the strongest semiprofessional team in Essex County. These guys were monsters, great mustachioed thirty-year-old bears, none under five foot ten or 165 pounds, who flexed their muscles and defiantly waved their big black bats.

In the Newburyport industrial league, the pitcher is

probably the least important member of the team. The whole idea is simply to lob the ball underhanded someplace where the batter *can* hit it, and then let the defense do the job. Since there is no umpire, there are no balls and strikes, walks, or called third strikes. (Only a swing-and-a-miss constituted a strike.) Stolen bases are outlawed. A tenth player, a short-centerfielder, is added and most of the outs are fly ball putouts, but if the ball goes over the fielder's head and *over the hill*, it's a ground-rule double.

Under those rules, I managed to lose 13–12, but pitched a complete game despite getting whacked in the left shoulder by a batted ball that gave me a sore shoulder for a week. I think the other guys kind of took it easy on us. I was a switch-hitter, changing from the left to the right side between pitches, and got on base once on a poor throw from short to first.

Newburyport ball was strictly for the fun of it, and I reexperienced that primal drive to play I thought had died the afternoon I wasted the home run. I had found an old picture of my kid brother in his Braves uniform, cute as the dickens. In the saloon after the game, we had another beer to celebrate the fact that we're in our thirties and out of shape but are still brothers and connected to ball, and by ball.

5

You can observe a lot by just watching.

—Yogi Berra

When I left home at seventeen to live in Boston and attend Boston University, it was 1963 and that city really offered all the cultural richnesses for which it's famous, with a tolerable level of urban stress. There was sleazy old Scollay Square full of drunken sailors, and everybody knew white folks didn't go to Roxbury (although I once drove for Town Taxi, headquartered behind Fenway Park, and took a cabload of George-Wallace-for-President campaign workers to the heart of the ghetto after they asked me to take them where they could "get some pussy"), but Cambridge was still refined and most parts of the city were safe to walk in at any hour. That, friends, was twenty years ago.

The sixties at Boston University were exciting, to say nothing of the true drama of it. In one electrifying coup after another, we placed a black militant into the office of Student Council president, myself into the editorship of the *B. U. News*, drove the Army ROTC off campus, forced the university president into early retirement, burned our draft cards, staged massive protests, sit-ins,

18

and marches, and got national attention for overturning the Massachusetts anti–birth control/anti-abortion laws and calling for Lyndon Johnson's impeachment.

Today, however, Boston is a kind of living hell to me, and not because the Red Sox don't win pennants. The steady decline in public education and rise in crime and urban decay have left a city in peril of losing its soul. The tableau that most affected me was the sight of schoolchildren uprooting the flowers in the Public Gardens while adults walked by unnoticing or pretending to ignore it. Some of these ten-year-olds have switchblades. And if Boston can't have flowers in the Public Gardens, can the Pope still be the Vicar of God on Earth?

In fact, it was the Pope who put me back in touch with Boston, when he appeared there in October 1979. As Religion Editor of *Mother Jones* magazine I followed the Holy Father on his American pilgrimage. One cold, dark, and raining October night—one of those New England nights that scare you to death about the coming winter, certainly a night to stay by the fireplace and avoid downtown Boston, which was cordoned off with Pope Rope—the people of Boston stood waiting for the smallest glimpse of the Prince of Rome. Despite the elements, hundreds of thousands lined the streets. After my photographer and I had seen the pontiff in his motorcade down Beacon Street, we (wisely) decided there was no point in getting wetter just to hear his sermon and see the Mass, so we repaired to the nearest spot to get out of the weather, a local gay bar called Streeter's on Cambridge Street.

There the leather boys, queens, fashion plates, working guys, and student gays of Boston had all fixated on the TV, where the Pope, larger than life, was holding forth. I interviewed the clientele: "Don't you realize that the Pope is against homosexuality?" "Ah, he'll change his mind before the government does."

Boston was probably a logical first stop for the Pope, being perhaps the American city most afflicted by the Catholic Church.

In 1981, the Catholic Bishops' Conference estimated that 40 percent of all United States Catholics "fall away" from the Church, some to return in later life, others to be replaced by earnest converts. But in Boston even the streets are named after monsignors and one is considered a Catholic, if raised that way, no matter how much a Christ-kicker, until death.

6

I'm sure you'd learn mathematics faster than I'd learn baseball.

—Albert Einstein

Fenway Park is as much a historical monument to Boston as the Bunker Hill Monument or Paul Revere's grave, and Boston is a town rich with monuments and great old structures. Fenway is so inner-city, it offers no parking at all and most patrons take the subway, which means they have to leave at 12:45 A.M. to catch the last train, even when the game's in the fourteenth inning and tied, with Gossage pitching and Rice at the plate.

I was lucky to find Fenway Park as the shining shrine of the game in my youth. The Red Sox, whether strong or weak, pennant-winners or also-rans, always have it going for them. Roger Angell called Fenway Park "the bijou of the American League." For any kid raised with Fenway as the shrine of ball, no other park will quite do. Its natural greenness, monster wall, and crazy-angled outfield corners (where the ball rattles around loose and out of view of the crowd, while Carl Yastrzemski stretches a double into a triple and the roar of the crowd echoes and rebounds and the stands shake!) are uniquely suited to exciting ball in an idyllic setting.

21

And the scene in the Boston press box is unsurpassed in the major leagues for authentic baseball atmosphere: the steady river of beer and shots of rye, and big black cigars, corned beef and cabbage in the press restaurant, hubbub and rumor, and the "Goodnight Irene" left-field Green Monster.

Fenway Park is still my favorite spot. For years there was a "White Fuel" sign in Kenmore Square, visible from inside the park, that featured a neon oil well that ejaculated white light into the evening sky over center field. When the game got boring or the Sox were down by five runs in the seventh, I'd gaze on that phallic illusion; it may have left me with lifetime associations between baseball and sex.

Anyway, I loved the Red Sox as a little kid loves his team—every fall I said "Wait 'til next year," and every spring I believed it had arrived. Would Williams hit .400? How were Malzone, Petrocelli, Conigliaro? I was "there" when Carl Yastrzemski played his first game, when Tony C. got beaned, and when Earl Wilson pitched his no-hitter; that is, even if I wasn't in the park, I lived these notable baseball events as markers of my days.

The Sox had a guy named Pumpsie Green who disappeared into the establishments of Kansas City with some regularity, occasionally taking a few other players with him on epic benders. The guys were rough and crude, and the Boston fans worse. At Fenway Park, I learned every ethnic slur and filthy epithet. Fathers brought sons into the male universe, a kind of initiation rite into the world of cigars, spit, beer, trash talk, and bigotry. Even today, you'll find few black faces in the crowd at Fenway, and fewer on the diamond. The Sox in 1980 fielded a twenty-five-man roster with twenty-three white guys, one brown, and one black.

New Englanders keep their Sox on, but part of the attitude is bitterly resentful and pessimistic. "The Sox have let us down so often," the fan thinks, "they might get close but they'll find a way to lose in the end." This gloomy fatalism must be rooted in the Puritan ethic, but it seems to affect the team. They *do* tend to lose in the end. No Sox fan will ever forget the seventh game of the 1975 World Series, when "they never should have taken out Willoughby"; or the one-game pennant playoff in 1978, which the Yankees won on a homer by "Why Bucky Dent?"

After that playoff, Boston was plunged into a citywide depression for months. Worse news followed: the team lost the services of Fred Lynn, Carlton Fisk, Butch Hobson, Rick Burleson, *et al.*, to trades and free agency, and was left fielding a lineup of strangers with names like Carney Lansford, Rich Gedman, Glenn Hoffman, and Dave Stapleton. Rice and Yaz remained, of course, but Bob Watson went to the Yanks and everybody in Boston said the Sox were finished.

Manager Don Zimmer, "the Gerbil," so named by Bill (Spaceman) Lee, was the target of the most vitriolic abuse I've ever witnessed from the fans and writers. I'm not saying he deserved it, but the team under Zimmer did disappoint everybody, always succumbing to mysterious diseases, and beating themselves in the end. A columnist for the *Boston Globe* described the demise of the Sox as akin to Greek tragedy.

But *tragedy* is a popular word in Boston. When Tony Conigliaro was beaned in 1967, it was a "tragedy." When Conigliaro later returned to the lineup, it was a "miracle." And recently, when Tony C. recovered from a six-month coma, it was an even bigger miracle, following a greater tragedy. The Red Sox are looking for miracles, and seemed by mid-'82 to be pulling one off. I know a nun in Dorchester who's praying for the Sox to win the World Series—she plans to tell the Pope it was a miracle if they do it. She's invoking the personal assistance of Fr. Junipero Serra, the eighteenth-century monk who founded the Carmelites in California and is up for sainthood *if*, if it can be proven he caused three miracles.

The '80 season opened inauspiciously for the Sox, who not only lost their first four games in Milwaukee but were bombed with grand-slam homers one after another. The public despair in Boston was so tangible you could cut it with a knife. Since I was wandering homelessly around the leagues, I gave careful consideration to re-basing in my native New England, but the Red Sox actually militated against it. I like to live where I can root for the home team and not suffer *too* much agony of defeat; this despite the fact that I lived in Seattle with the hapless Mariners for years, loving that wet city and bearing with the young team.

The cause of agony may be increased by Boston writers who love to heap scorn and abuse on losing managers and players. In 1980, when Don ("the Gerbil") was in office, the heat was getting out of hand. When the team did well, which it did often, the writers acted surprised; when it failed, they kept saying, "I told you so."

7

It's about
the ball,
the bat,
and the mitt.
Ball hits
bat, or it
hits mitt.
Bat doesn't
hit ball, bat
meets it.
Ball bounces
off bat, flies
air, or thuds
ground (dud)
or it
fits mitt.

—May Swenson, from
"Analysis of Baseball"

If there's an easy way to get from Boston to New York, I haven't found it in twenty years of looking. You can drive the throughways and interstates and pay a fortune in tolls and take the risks of overcrowded roads in bad repair and the ineluctable whoosh of feverish civilization and bad air that leads into the heart of Manhattan. You can take a train and hope it gets there on time and that the air conditioning or heating doesn't break down, and most of all that the bar holds out through any crisis. You can fly the shuttle and have to get to and from the airports on either end, which can take almost as long as making the trip overland. Or you can take a bus, and greet New York through its least appealing porthole, the Port Authority. Buses between major Eastern cities also attract a proportion of the mentally crippled population. It's a rare one that doesn't have an unshaven wino hacking and coughing in the back row, hoping for the chance to lie down; or a bag lady with stories; sullen youth; stoned longhair on since San Francisco, whose pint bottle of bourbon goes rolling down the aisle toward the driver, who barks "No smokin' marijuana on dis bus!"

Of these grim alternatives, we usually choose the drive. At least in one's own car, one can listen to the ballgame, stop for a greasy burger. I've heard some of the best talk of my life in old jalopies between New York and Boston. And when the vehicle lands in the big town, you've got a personal escape mechanism with which to blow town when the heat gets too much. I usually arrive in New York at sundown and leave at dawn, or the moment before it. That last hour of darkness is the magic zone in which the junkies and insomniacs have a fleeting moment to slip away unnoticed.

When a good friend left town for Australia, I found myself the shocked proprietor of a two-bedroom apartment with Siamese cat and Sony Trinitron baseball action, on the corner of Christopher and Bleecker Streets in the Village. As any New Yorker knows, there's a world of difference between visiting the town and having your own place to hide in. The apartment became my personal and inviolable sanctuary from the madness of the streets. I even put off all callers with a tape-recorded message, and refused to answer the electronic door buzzer in the night.

Ever, there were the Yanks and Mets on the tube. One is a moneyed industry bloated with pride, ego, nasty innuendo, fans who have been properly called animals in a park appropriately called a zoo. The other is, or was, a pathetically undertalented group kept out of last place in the National League East only by the Chicago Cubs. Nonetheless, I embraced the Mets and wished them well and liked going out to Shea Stadium to sit in the sunshine and engage in the rituals.

Yankee Stadium is the house that Ruth built and ruthlessness sustained. Nobody can fault George Steinbrenner, the flamboyant owner, for spending all the money necessary to build a perennial-champion team, or for hiring and firing managers at a furious pace. But his constant meddling and adolescent ego and endless beefing and criticizing his own players is an act that wears a bit thinner every year. Steinbrenner's worth his weight in press clippings, but when he hogs the limelight and his little internecine wars get more press than the game itself, he's operating contrary to the best interests of baseball.

Too much has already been written about Steinbrenner, including several unauthorized books. Sparky Lyle's book *The Bronx Zoo* has all the salient, vicious gossip if you can stomach it. The Yankees themselves, great menacing Red Sox–killers of my youth, are no longer the stable, established, can't-be-beat kings of baseball. They change personnel so quickly there's no telling who will be playing for them by the time you read this. Every player is expendable at the whim of King George, as the fans found out when even Reggie Jackson was sent packing. "Mr. October" hit a home run in his first game against the Yanks as a California Angel, and the New York fans literally shouted Steinbrenner out of the park with a lusty, coordinated chant of "Steinbrenner Sucks!" The Bronx Zoo, indeed. Yankee Stadium is a dangerous place when the fans get drunk and pugnacious, and it's in a grim neighborhood to boot.

Still, my first visit to Yankee Stadium was an awe-inspiring experience for me. The park, since its renovation in the mid-seventies, is simply grand, big, gleaming, overwhelming. The latticework outfield walls, the famous right-field third deck overhang, the air itself charged with auras of Ruth, Gehrig, Mantle, Maris, murderers' rows of the past—all of that and more made me feel very small in Yankee Stadium, and very afraid. This is the Big Show, these guys are the Best. They've been stomping my heart since I was an innocent schoolboy. This is, as the nightly repeated Sinatra song goes, "New Yawk, New Yawk!" They don't fuck around. They play an angry, aggressive kind of ball, and I felt that I personally (all 115 pounds of me) was the intended victim.

Nevertheless, I date the demise of the Yanks from that 1980 season, and from a specific date, at-bat, and hit: that being, of course, George Brett's three-run homer off Goose Gossage in the League Championship Series Game 3. That gave the Kansas City Royals a clean sweep of the Yanks and the pennant. You'll recall that Brett hit .390 that year, and that Gossage was the most feared relief pitcher in baseball. When "the Goose is loose," opposing batters want to go home.

So when Brett hit that three-run homer, I was also the victor, triumphant. The moment would have been less thrilling had it been any other batter than Brett, any other pitcher than the Goose. It was power against power, and the best man won.

In every way, Shea is the antithesis of Yankee Stadium, and maybe that's why it became my baseball home in New York City.

I enjoyed Shea Stadium more because there was no tension for me, no painful memories of childhood defeats, nothing but the sweet, ineffectual, lovable-loser Mets (a team nobody could really despise, but also a team that hasn't done much since 1969 except provoke a lot of yawning). A Mets game in recent years has been a pleasant, low-key, easygoing experience. There's seldom any difficulty getting a last-minute ticket, as attendance is only fair. Shea Stadium is a picturesque, pretty ball park with orange seats, orange everywhere, in fact, where the fans are friendly and accustomed to losing, not winning.

A lot of girl- and boy-watching goes on in Shea Stadium when the summer heat brings people out in little more than skin. Whatever your fantasy, it's there walking around at the ball park in shorts, with or without topping. Every team has players who are objects of massive sexual desire coming from the stands. Guys like Jim Palmer turn this attraction into good money doing underwear ads, and after his 1978 homer winning the pennant for the Yankees, Bucky Dent even authorized a poster of himself in short shorts and nothing else, wielding his great bat.

The Mets, to be fair, are on a self-improvement course

since Doubleday and Company bought the team in 1980. But they seem to still have a ways to go. The Mets are the only team I can think of that created a player famous (and *still* famous, through TV beer ads) for being so utterly terrible: Marvelous Marv Throneberry! And the Mets *do* hold the world's record for losses in a season, 120. (One of these days, though, they may lose that mark to the pathetic Minnesota Twins, now being patiently disassembled by owner Calvin Griffith.)

8

No outfielder is a real workman unless he can turn
his back on the ball, run his legs off and take the
catch over his shoulder. Backpedaling outfielders
get nowhere.

—Joe DiMaggio,
"How to Play the Outfield"

My two experiences at Yankee Stadium had left me
hopeful of never returning there. The Yankees are the
only team I visited who had different press boxes for
different-caliber writers. The A-box guys, the daily jour-
nalists, for example, got better seats, food, and booze.
The B-level wretches, myself included, were off to the
side without so much as a Coke or hot dog. "You think
Steinbrenner's gonna buy you a beer?" snorted a fellow
wretch from some Jersey weekly. I realized I'd been
spoiled by good treatment from nicer guys. "Nice guys
finish last": I guess no better example exists than Calvin
Griffith, owner of the Minnesota Twins, who fed the
press steak and whiskey and enormous breakfasts and
lunches. And whose team I was to visit next in their old
haunt: Bloomington Stadium. I had run away from New
York in a 1961 Rambler American purchased for two

hundred dollars that made it to Minneapolis, and no farther.

Bloomington Stadium, technically called Metropolitan Stadium, was one of those great old wooden ball parks like Shibe, Polo Grounds, or Ebbets Field, that in 1980 was being abandoned and since then has been elevated to holy status in our memories. In 1982 the Twins moved into the downtown Hubert H. Humphrey MetroDome, or, to some Minneapolis wags, the HumpDome. In 1980 the old park was still there, a haven of mine as it had been throughout the seventies. There, in the glory days, the Twins had sent Rod Carew and Lyman Bostock and Larry Hisle up in the middle of the order.

The park was comfortable in a creaky sort of way, seats were cheap, and you could get a great tan under the blazing midsummer sun. Doubles and triples slammed against those venerable wooden outfield walls—the Twins had been known for great hitting since the days of Harmon Killebrew, who now does color commentary for the Oakland A's TV network—the club had a great farm system, and the fans were loyal and true. The hot dogs were savory and the peanuts salty and you could get oceans of beer at a very reasonable price. Everything about the park and the team was tailored to the sensible, blue-collar attitude of the land of ten thousand lakes.

I can't even go *on* like this. Nineteen-eighty was my last year there and I miss that old dump badly. And the Twins too were going downhill.

Stops on the way to Bloomington Stadium: Pittsburgh, Cleveland, Detroit, Milwaukee, Cincinnati, all of them industrial, gray, not great towns for a stranger, but tabernacles of old baseball heart. I'd blow in, catch the game, get the hell out of town by nightfall. I skirted Chicago completely, postponing it until August when the weather would be properly unbearable.

I stayed with a friend in Minneapolis who did a little dealing and was later found with a woman, unfortunately several days dead, in his apartment. I don't know how she met her end: my friend had never seemed violent in the least but coke eradicates memory and nobody may ever know what really happened.

9

I should of stood in bed.

—Joe Jacobs, 1935

California is blessed with terrific weather, stunning views, and sophistication in a natural setting; and it is cursed with tourists, relentless developers, high prices, and that particular hot-tub style of decadence that is definitely not for the faint of heart. Only in New York City and California have I found a world of *constant* partying, occult boozing, recreational drugging, and of course sex. But California sex is, well, not just your good old, down-dirty sex, but some kind of mellow cousin that leaves you wondering if anything happened at all. For Pete's sake, don't take it seriously, but do have fun. Fun is very important in America, and especially in California. Too much fun and not enough real pleasure, though, is hard on the kidneys, liver, blood pressure, lungs, and brain.

Two great places to go in L.A. are Dodger Stadium and Disneyland. On the last weekend in August of 1978, the San Francisco Giants opened a four-game series against the Dodgers with the Giants in first place in the National League West by one-half game over the Dodg-

34

ers. Simultaneously, I arrived by car in L.A. with a woman friend and four kids—mine, hers, and other people's. We settled into a friend's comfortable house, set the kids loose in the swimming pool, raided the walk-in liquor closet, and parked ourselves in front of the wide-screen cable TV to pig out on the four-game Giants/Dodgers series. The games themselves had long been sold out.

Thursday night, in the first game, the Dodgers humiliated the Giants and routed Vida Blue, winning 12–2 and taking over first place by a half-game.

We and the kids arrived at Disneyland at noon the following day. My woman friend had a migraine. "My mom *always* has headaches when it's time to go to Disneyland," her eight-year-old daughter chirped in the back seat.

After a few hours in Disneyland, it's hard to remember you're still in the United States, or for that matter on Earth. After lunch in Captain Hook's ship and a trip through Space Mountain, the illusion of a "kingdom" is complete. At nine o'clock, they turned down the lights and the booming voice of old Walt Disney introduced a spectacular fireworks display "to honor America." "Gee, that Walt Disney sure is *generous*," my seven-year-old son enthused from under his mouse-ears.

Friday night's second Dodgers/Giants game came on the portable radio just then and I followed it assiduously while keeping guard on two kids while the others got lost. I made such a spectacle of myself leaping for joy at every Giant hit that the kids disowned me: "I'm not with *him*," their eyes said. The Giants lost again, falling a game and a half off pace. I went into deepest despair. We stayed until after midnight, when the last kids finally appeared. "Where have you been?" I shouted. They very sweetly listed all twenty or so rides. We staggered through the exit gates laden with souvenirs and I drove an hour on three L.A. freeways while the youngsters snored. Back home, I poured myself a tumbler of vodka over ice and swilled it down in two or three gulps, but felt no effect. When I woke up Saturday morning, the room was swimming, lights whirling, music playing, and for a terrible moment I thought I was still in Disneyland.

Saturday afternoon, the Giants bounced back to beat the Dodgers and get within a half-game again. After losing the first two games, the Giants were in a must-win situation if they were not to blow their season-long pennant fever. They had a spirit in '78 that they haven't had since. They'd been in first place all season thanks to winning more one-run contests than any other team; to superb relief pitching by Gary Lavelle and Randy Moffit; and to home-run heroics by Mike Ivie and Willie McCovey. I was in a post-Disneyland stupor, but watched the game on the wide-screen TV and was astonished when the Giants came from behind to win.

That meant that Sunday's fourth and final game was to be crucial. If the Giants could win it, they'd regain first place and leave L.A. triumphant. If they lost, the Dodgers would have a game-and-a-half lead on them, a lead from which (historically speaking) the Giants were unlikely to recover.

Saturday night, box-seat tickets for Sunday afternoon's game miraculously appeared. Our host, an industrial magnate, controlled four season tickets on the third-base line, and at the last minute one of the four people had to cancel out. That left a single ticket available. My woman friend and the kids all agreed that I deserved the honor of this single ticket since I'd done such yeoman service at Disneyland! I wound up on the third-base line for the fourth and final game of the series. Dodger Stadium was washed in sunshine, verdant green field bouncing off the blue sky, and we ate Dodger Dogs with onions, sauerkraut, mustard, and relish. Ball park food is generally so bad that it can kill you, but Dodger Dogs are exceptional. I could scarcely digest anyway, I was an away-team fan in the hated enemy's park for the first time in the heat of an incredible pennant race. The Giants, perennial losers, were high on Vida Blue, in his first season with S.F., and old McCovey extending his record for left-handed home runs, and Ivie pinch-hitting grand slams. The Dodgers, accustomed to winning their division, were wondering why they hadn't already opened up a considerable lead.

The Dodgers, for their part, were simply the Best in the West and had been for some time. Their great and established infield of Cey, Russell, Lopes, and Garvey was in its prime. I feared those four hitters in particular, along with Dusty Baker, as I had once feared the Yankees of old. It was almost an uncomfortable parallel to my youth. Once with Boston, now with San Francisco. Once humiliated by New York, now by L.A.

The Dodgers also had pitching—and what pitching! Tommy John was at his best. Burt Hooton never smiled and so was nicknamed "Happy." The kid named Bob Welch was destined for a World Series moment that any pitcher would remember forever—striking out Reggie Jackson at a crucial moment.

Dodger Stadium, like Yankee Stadium, was awesome . . . but in a clean-jean California kind of way. It's Hollywood. It's chic. And it's a white folks' delight taken

37

by eminent domain from a Mexican community (Chavez Ravine) twenty years ago.

The game turned out to be one of those dreams that you relish when you're reveling in it but rarely see come true. I was pleased to find myself sitting next to two equally rabid Giant fans, amazed when the Giants came back again and again to send the game to twelve innings, and astonished when they used *all* their relief pitchers and had to send in a starter, Ed Halicki, to save the victory. The final score was 9−8 in favor of my heroes, and I'm lucky to have survived the pummeling and embraces from my hysterical mates. My host, a Dodger fan, graciously said, "The Giants appear to be the team of destiny."

That might have been my happiest L.A. experience, as well as the last great moment for the Giants. They folded disastrously in September and wound up in third place but that August of 1978 found Los Angeles stunned by the new Giant Strength. I headed north from L.A. humming bars of the popular disco hit "Giant Fever." *"I'm a believer!"*

10

A sensational event was changing from the brown
suit to the gray the contents of his pocket. He was
earnest about these objects. They were of eternal
importance, like baseball . . .

—Sinclair Lewis,
from *Babbitt*

But let me stay in the past, and follow the Giants—*my*
team—into the 1979 season.

The pressure had built toward Opening Day. The
burning issue for the Giants at the start of the 1979
season was whether Willie McCovey, age thirty-nine and
obviously slowing down but still capable of power and a
crowd favorite, or Mike Ivie, a young slugger who later
developed mental and psychological fatigue, would play
first base. The *San Francisco Chronicle* conducted a
reader poll in which fans voted for one or the other. Ivie
won.

Old baseball players become venerable. They remain
part of the fan's life for years after they have stopped
playing. Great moments in ball are forever enshrined in
our collective consciousness. The great old stars of the
game eventually achieve dignity and stature in the public eye. Joe DiMaggio sells Mr. Coffee, and for you, Joe,

I'd almost buy one; you were the one who really loved Marilyn. You're the one who brings flowers to her grave. Ted Williams, you can sell me Sears camping gear any day. Willie Stargell, you want money for sickle-cell anemia research, and I'll contribute. I ask myself only where the young kids are in baseball who will eventually become venerable. Will John "the Count" Montefusco become venerable? I rather doubt it . . . not to single out the Count, mind you.

McCovey lost the poll and Ivie started the game on opening day at San Francisco. A record crowd watched the game go down to the bottom of the ninth with two outs, the bags empty, and the score tied, 2–2. When McCovey came up to pinch-hit, the crowd went wild; and when he singled sharply to right center, he got a second standing ovation. Willie'd looked bad on the first pitch, swinging and missing and tumbling into the dirt with a thud. But he connected with the round ball squarely, and immediately left the game for a pinch-runner. The next batter, a third-string catcher named John Tamargo, hit a home run over the right field fence and the Giants won, 4–2. Tamargo was the hero of the day but soon thereafter was traded to Montreal, while Willie Mac went on to retire as the greatest left-handed home run hitter in baseball.

In his final year, 1980, McCovey got standing ovations at every ball park in the National League.

McCovey joins Willie Mays and Hank Aaron in the select group of black Hall of Famers (Mac will be eligible for induction in 1985) who never quite got their just deserts from baseball. Aaron's breaking of Babe Ruth's all-time home run record was marred by racist taunts and threats. They've yet to have a Willie Mays Day at

40

Candlestick Park, and baseball commissioner Bowie Kuhn has barred Mays from the game since Willie took a public-relations job with an Atlantic City casino. Kuhn doesn't seem to care that some club owners, like George Steinbrenner, own race horses and hang around tracks.

Well, nobody promised me the nicest dream in the world. But baseball fills the long hours of waiting.

11

―――――――

. . . when I grew to the grave maturity of 11 or 12 I
saw, one crisp October morning, in the back Textile
field, a great pitching performance by a husky
strangely old-looking 14-year-older, or 13—a very
heroic-looking boy in the morning . . . his name
was Boldieu, it immediately stuck in my mind with
Beaulieu—street where I learned to cry and be
scared of the dark and of my brother for many
years (till almost 10)—this proved to me that *all
my life wasn't black.*

—Jack Kerouac,
from *Doctor Sax*

The road from Big Sur to San Francisco seems tortu-
rously long and winding if you stay on the coast route,
and ugly as sin if you go inland through San Jose and the
ten-mile Coyote strip detour on 101. But on a Sunday
morning, with the sun shining brightly on Monterey
County hills and beaches, and the avowed mission of
meeting Vida Blue at the Giants' Boosters mixer at a
restaurant on Maiden Lane, the miles flew under me.
Picked up a hitchhiker at Salinas and took him to the
Hollister exit. Decided on the inland route after noticing
black clouds forming over Castroville on the coast side.
Weather bureau forecast fair skies.

Prunedale, San Juan Bautista, Gilroy, and on to the famous Coyote strip, I drove through the brilliant morning thinking about Vida Blue. I've often seen him work and everybody knows Vida is a good pitcher but I've seen great pitchers I wouldn't travel a mile to meet. You meet baseball players outside the players' gate, or at shopping centers. You can also go to banquets where speeches are made and the players as often as not seem embarrassed and out of place. In general, meeting baseball players off the field serves only to diminish their supernatural grace in our eyes, to reduce them to human beings.

But Vida Blue is another story. He actually transmits love waves and positive thought patterns right over TV or from the printed page. He must be one of the nicest guys you could ever want to meet. He doesn't complain, but is right there cheering everybody on; always smiling, a spiritual force for the Giants. Can this guy be *that* good?

I wanted to meet him, just for half a minute, nothing heavy, small talk maybe, just to thank him for rekindling my own spirit when times were toughest. I remembered the World Series games with the A's, the All-Star game he worked for the American League, the way he dealt with Finley, the aborted deals to Cincinnati and elsewhere, the sad season of 1977 when he seemed to be working for the A's with no heart or spirit left, and the tremendous enthusiasm he brought with him to the Giants in 1978. Through it all, you knew this guy was special.

All this was going through my mind as the freeway ended at Coyote and turned into the narrow strip of produce stands, gas stations, Mexican cafés. It started to rain, and I congratulated myself on having fixed my windshield wipers a few days earlier. I turned them on and they worked fine for six or eight miles. Then they suddenly stopped, blowing a fuse that also operated my brake lights, gas gauge, turn signals, and other functions.

I've driven without wipers before, and as you know it's difficult but possible, assuming the rainfall is light and visibility good. But this was the kind of driving downpour through which nobody could drive. Period. The rain came down in sheets, pounded the earth and made great rivers alongside the road. I moved into the rightmost lane, hazard lights blinking, and pulled into the first service station I found.

The kindly old man looked at my burned-out Fiat fuse and shook his head sadly. Couldn't replace a Fiat fuse, but he did show me how to wrap it in tinfoil and thus make it a functioning fuse again, if dangerously incapable of blowing. It restored my lights and turn signals but didn't fix the wipers. The old man said the next station down the line usually had a mechanic on duty.

I took the shoulder lane at twenty mph, hazards blinking furiously as bumper-to-bumper traffic roared past me through the gale, which showed no signs of letting up.

The new station featured three identically jump-suited teen-aged boys who found my situation hilarious. One of them suggested I "hire a nigger to sit on your hood and run them by hand." The other two laughed as if it was the greatest joke they'd heard since *Animal House*. One added that I could drive with my left hand outside the car and run the wipers myself. The other two went into convulsions. The prospects for seeing Vida Blue got dimmer and dimmer.

I decided to leave the car at the Morons' Gas Station, but they wouldn't allow me to. Boss wouldn't like it. I wasn't carrying enough cash to pay a tow truck. Trapped in a Fiat, I kept the heater on and watched the rain destroy my day. After an hour, it was either drive on or go crazy, so I proceeded in the now familiar shoulder-lane technique to the next gas station and cantina, the last before the freeway would resume. Chickens running around underfoot. Here I gave up for good, locked the car and kicked it ("goddamn so-called Italian engineering"), and started hitchhiking.

But I gave up hitchhiking ten years ago, and I guess I forgot how to do it, because nobody stopped for me. I was a small, wet guy with a Giants hat and thin Giants jacket, carrying a paper bag, standing out in the pouring rain in front of a Mexican café. Obviously a wacko. I tried to preserve sanity by focusing on Vida Blue. Would Vida Blue let a little thing like a windshield wiper stand between him and victory?

Finally there was nothing left to do but return to the chickens, take the car, and drive through the rain. It was five o'clock and getting dark in San Jose. I had been due in San Francisco at three. A temporary letup in the rain made it possible to slip north, mile by agonizing mile. But the deluge resumed in Santa Clara, and finally darkness fell and I had to abandon the car in a bus stop on El Camino between Millbrae and San Mateo. I ducked into a corner saloon and called the SAM-Trans bus people to determine the time of the next bus into the city, then sipped a vodka tonic or two while watching the Harlem Globetrotters on TV. Laughed like crazed. It had been eight hours on the road already, and another hour to come on the bus, and I couldn't be sure that Vida and the Giants hadn't already gone home.

I got off at Fifth and Mission and found Maiden Lane with the help of a woman who turned out to be a man. Two tall guys in Giants uniforms admitted me to the restaurant even though I didn't have a Boosters membership card because, as they put it, I was wearing team colors. They opened the doors and I was confronted with a solid wall of chattering, smoking, drinking human bodies. No ball players in sight, and no Vida Blue. Somebody pointed out the back of outfielder Jack Clark's head.

I circulated around the party and yes, the players were there, but you can't just stand and gawk at a guy when he's trying to eat his steak. Upstairs in a loft lounge, one of those home-movie-screen TVs showed a film of last season's Giant accomplishments, which the audience vastly enjoyed. Big cheers for Mike Ivie. I sat next to an elderly black lady who reminisced about Willie Mays while she nursed a glass of white wine. "What a man he was!" she said. I ordered a vodka tonic several times, but over an hour passed and they never brought my drink.

"It's nothin' if you don't need it, honey," she advised. I ate a bag of ball-park peanuts.

The thought of my Fiat in the bus stop in Millbrae was never far from my mind. I began to feel sorry for the Fiat, and for cursing it. Clearly there was to be no chance to meet Vida Blue, I thought, and I had better rescue the car and get back home by any means necessary. I gathered up some Giants souvenirs and put them in my wet paper bag on top of the now-pathetic 1972 *Sports Illustrated* with Vida on the cover and assorted other Blueiana.

I decided to take the back door exit so as to circumvent the Giants fans engaging in shoulder-to-shoulder celebration and hot-stove league gossip. It was good to see San Francisco backing its team, but I didn't want to see any more of San Francisco itself. It had finally stopped raining, and I wanted to be in my bed forgetting to worry about Mike Ivie, John the Count, Halicki and Knepper, the great Madlock, McCovey, Clark and Evans, and, of course, V. B.

I found him by accident on my way out. He was in the back standing by the kitchen door, and not even surrounded but just talking with a guy in a business suit, smiling, drinking orange juice.

A moment of panic. But a smile from Vida breaks the ice and after that he's just human, and warm. We shake hands. He says:

"Hey, man, you're soaking wet. What you got in that bag?"

"I got all your old stuff for you to autograph."

"(Bleep), you really *do* got the old stuff! Well, that's really nice of you, man." (He laughs, signs the autographs.)

"I hope you have a great year and that the Giants win the pennant!"

"We're goin' for the *gold*, man!"

Wow. "Goin' for the gold." It is my new mantra. I walk out of the restaurant chanting it over and over in my mind. Goin' for the gold. You wish this man thirty victories a year and an ERA of 1.13. He says, "You might think I'm crazy, but I think we can win our division with the team we've got right now." But nobody thinks he's crazy. We also believe.

12

Baseball is fathers and sons. Football is brothers
beating each other up in the backyard.
—Donald Hall, from
Fathers Playing Catch with Sons

Families just aren't what they used to be in America's
new age. In my circle of friends, it's a rare child who's
being raised by both natural parents. There's usually a
stepparent involved, or if the parent is single friends
may serve as surrogates. So, though I can't always be
with my son, I do spend time with other peoples' kids in
a semiparental role. If you like kids, you find them
everywhere, all looking for some attention and love. So
we make new families, have birthday parties, celebrate
holidays just like regular families though we aren't "related."

But the best part is every summer when I pick up my
son for six weeks, more or less, of fun and games and
regular father-and-son domestic living. I see him at
other times of the year, when I can get to the distant
Pacific Northwest, described by Kevin Kerrane as "the
vast centerfield of the United States of Baseball." I'm
one of the army of single fathers who live at a distance

from their children. The phenomenon has given rise to entire industries.

There is something called a Noncustodial Parent season, and that is summer. Conventionally, kids visit the noncustodial for a month or two. All the airlines are adept at handling unaccompanied minors, and they haven't lost a kid yet to my knowledge, but they do charge full adult fare, increasing their revenues greatly. Unaccompanied kids by the millions are zinging around on airplanes from June through August and again at Christmas. The arrangements are usually made via long-distance call, and the kid naturally calls the custodial parent once a week or something, so the phone company reaps huge new revenues. And think of the business gains in the entertainment industry! The noncustodial parent must provide treats like movies, amusement parks, zoos, restaurants, presents, comic books, and outings to the ocean, mountains, and urban cultural attractions like "opera in the park" and a good jazz festival, so as to give the kid a good time and some intellectual stimulation, a whale of a summer vacation, and to assuage said parent's guilt about not being around in the kid's life for ten months of the year.

That 1980 season, I bought a 1969 Dodge camper van for fourteen hundred dollars from a guy in Berkeley and, grabbing the kid, set off into the sunrise in search of baseball, camping, comic books, and general vacation fun. The vehicle was more than grand enough for our every wish. It slept four, with a double bed for me and single for him; a two-burner stove that ran on propane; small refrigerator; reading lamps, shelves, tables; and a nifty sink with running hot water. The only thing it lacked was a toilet, and as that can be an urgent need with small kids, we parked as close as possible to the conveniences in KOA Kampgrounds and state parks all over the West.

Invited to a writers' literary rodeo on July 4 at Livingston, Montana, we bravely pioneered across Idaho and into the Rockies, stopping for ice cream or swimming or to watch ballgames on TV in motel rooms or on video in the van. I could not but feel this was one of the times in my life when I was unaccountably blessed with tremendous good fortune. Every love and tenderness surrounded me. My little boy, just six and already a tiny man with a big heart, was guardian angel to our travels.

All the rooms at the Chico Hot Springs resort, where the writers and movie stars gathered, were rented, so we camped out in the parking lot. Days we soaked in natural hot springs and nights dined in the four-star restaurant.

When my kid and I get together, it's a kind of paradise for us, stirred stronger by our temporary deprivation of each other. "This is the way it ought to be." It was one of those beautiful dreams that can't go on forever, and when it ended the crash was abrupt. The Dodge van blew its valves. Our self-indulgence on the road had left us without the cost of a major engine overhaul, nine hundred dollars. Ruefully, we had to swap the camper for a functioning Jeep station wagon that would at least get us out of Livingston free of charge.

"It's not as good as the camper," he said.

"But it runs," I sighed.

We never discussed it again. A week or so later, the Jeep was overtaken in eastern Washington by great clouds of volcanic ash from the May 18 Mount St. Helen's eruption, which rolled across the desert like a cloud of menacing locusts. Visibility dropped from good to almost zero in seconds. We were left suddenly, completely, in the dark. Desperately I pumped the brakes to avoid hitting the car in front of us.

But on the day of the eruption itself, a Sunday, nothing had disturbed our Peter Pan universe. I'd been camping with my son and his sister, my stepdaughter. Those titles are a little pompous. What I mean is, I was camping with the kids in the wilds of Index, Washington, about fifty miles away from Mount St. Helen's, when it blew up. We were cooking hot dogs and salad for the vegetarians among us, drank lemonade, and told ghost stories by the fire, all those divine pleasures of childhood. Some other family in the campground had fireworks. The grown-ups stayed up a bit later by the fire, drinking beer and tequila and sharing a joint, keeping an eye on the lighted campers and motor homes, where the wee ones slept peacefully.

Aah. Picking flowers in the wilderness and skipping rocks off the Skykomish River, we didn't learn of the mountain's eruption until two hours later. When we returned to the KOA Kampground, everybody was around the color TV in the tiny store and registration office, watching footage of the big blast that had rocked the world just to our south.

Volcanic eruptions are ill winds if they blow nobody good. Some friends in Seattle published a book about Mount St. Helen's that made *The New York Times* bestseller list and turned a small company into a success. The Seattle Mariners suddenly went into a winning streak, and I was able somehow to endure the plastic confines of the Kingdome with its brown-shirted attendants, lost echoes, hanging speakers, expensive beer, and impossible-to-see video screen, for the sake of the game. The minor league Spokane Indians became the first baseball team to have several games "volcanoed out," and while the team was staying in Seattle, because Spokane was closed to travel, its uniforms were stolen from the parking lot of a topless tavern.

13

Owning the Yankees is like owning the Mona Lisa.
—George Steinbrenner

In Seattle, they have the finest play-by-play announcers in the business, Dave Niehaus and Ken Wilson. It's worth a trip to the Northwest to hear them. Making the Mariners sound exciting is no mean task. They have finished last, or second to last, through the first five years. That was to be expected, but when they hadn't shown any improvement by the end of 1981, Seattle fans got discouraged indeed and the attendance figures at the Kingdome dipped to pathetic league-wide lows. It's actually more entertaining to hear the game described by Niehaus and Wilson over the radio than to go in person to the airless Dome, where you can't smoke and can't see the game well thanks to poor lighting.

But Dave and Ken are boundlessly cheerful, personable announcers who always look on the bright side of the Mariners' continuing effort to climb to respectability. At times when I'm away from Seattle, I actually miss hearing their voices, their patented ways of describing a game. As in, "*Mr.* Bruce Bochte then slammed a three-run homer that *kissed* the third deck of the right-field stands."

Once or twice, I've had the pleasure of watching the Mariners *and* hearing Dave and Ken's commentary without having to be in Seattle or the Kingdome. In August 1980, the Red Sox had just won nine games in a row and were facing a home four-game weekend series with the Mariners, who that year finished with the worst record in the major leagues. The hapless Mariners had never won a series in Fenway Park. *Seattle P-I* baseball reporter J Michael Kenyon (that's right, no period on the J) wrote: "The Mariners couldn't successfully promote a live sex act." Over the years they've had a few good hitters (Bochte, Meyer, Zisk, Horton, Ruppert Jones) but miserable pitching that fared even worse for playing in the cheap-homer Dome. They also had an ownership problem until George Argyros bought the team from its original six-man ownership team, which couldn't get together to decide anything. Argyros' current approach with the Mariners is, apparently, to spend as little as possible.

The Mariners have lost a lot of games in a lot of ways, and in Boston they were viewed as a patsy, an easy mark. The Boston press felt simply that the Red Sox would and *must* take all four games from the Seattle Mariners in order to have *any* hope of catching up with the hated Yanks.

Niehaus and Wilson were in the Seattle booth preparing for the opening game of the series. We exchanged pleasantries about the team, my book, the season. I had my White Owls and shot glass of whiskey, impeccable score card with starting lineups, selection of sharp pencils, etc., and took a seat in the press box, separated from my Seattle buddies by only a pane of glass. It was a balmy night with the windows open, and I could hear

Niehaus' voice floating on the summer night as Danny Meyer blasted a three-run homer in the top of the first inning to put Seattle ahead, 3–0:

"It's a drive to DEEP right field, Miller's going back, back, BACK, to the WARNING track, to the WALL, and it will fly, fly, FLY AWAY!!!!"

A thrill and a half, folks, if you've ever been there. The lowly Seattles went on to crush the Red Sox by a lopsided score, and that night in the clubhouse, bubbly merriment ensued. I avoided the Boston clubhouse entirely, and instead went out drinking with some Ancient Mariners. I've always thought the team should hire up all the old great players like McCovey and Stargell and Buddy Harrelson, guys too old to make it with better teams but loved by the fans, and literally promote the "ancient Mariner" idea. Hell, they've got nothing to lose.

Gaylord Perry is their current token Ancient Mariner, and they've had others. Willie Horton . . . *Diego Segui!* But wouldn't it be neat if they fielded a whole lineup of former greats still in the game? Well, I guess not. They need young players to develop into stars for them. The problem is that as soon as the young player becomes a star, his salary demands far outstrip the Mariners' willingness to pay, and he goes packing. Ex-Mariners like Tom Paciorek, Ruppert Jones, and Dave Collins are now top players on better clubs.

The Mariners won again on Saturday, lost on Sunday, and won on Monday, completing a three-out-of-four winning series, the first series they'd ever won at Fenway Park, and pushing the Red Sox a full six games behind the Yankees while driving fans and writers both into a despondency that never let up throughout September.

The Mariners, already long out of contention, enjoyed

perhaps their happiest weekend on the road. Outfielder Tom Paciorek, joking in the clubhouse after the series, said, "The Mariners will win the pennant because all the other teams will be disqualified for drug abuse."

The local joke in the bars was that the Red Sox would be moved to the Philippines and renamed the Manila Folders.

Jim Rice and Tony Perez, the only players of color on the Red Sox, went into the trainers' room after every game and refused to commingle with either the press or their fellow players.

People said there wasn't much chance of the world surviving past the year 2000 anyway.

14

Van Mungo liked to drink a bit. Anything. Even hair tonic.
—Leo Durocher

The homelessness of ball: The player gets drafted out of high school, in a properly military fashion, and is sent away from home for the first time in his life, not to some fancy school with dorms and girls and laundry service but to Great Falls, Montana, or Tuscaloosa, or Tacoma, for long bus rides, lousy food, and faint accommodation. If he's lucky enough to work his way up to the big show, the dives become first-class hotels and the buses chartered jets, and he can live on the road in cushy idleness. After the first few times around, he knows all the bars and joints and there's simply nothing to do a lot.

So too the avid fan that summer of '80: while the players got to be "home" at least half the time, I was on the road at all times, fashioning home in a tiny camper van, making a family of it as best I could, drinking too much, wondering why I couldn't stop, stay, settle down, realizing it takes two to do that number and I'm alone, and baseball is my mistress.

Even my best friends couldn't take my baseball excess, wearing headphones at parties, not taking phone calls (except during commercials), turning on the TV sets at friends' houses, always having to wait to catch me between innings. It can be a long wait. The game is theoretically endless, and for nonfans literally so.

Having dropped off my kid, I headed east again to Chicago, to meet my pal Barry Gifford, a writer formerly from Chicago and now from Berkeley. Gifford knows a *lot* about the Cubs. He's one of those driven Cub fans who has stuck with the team through decades of unprecedented mediocrity.

It was the hottest, most humid time of the year—dead-end August—and we planned to sit around Wrigley Field drinking, sweating, and having a hell of a good time.

Well, it didn't quite turn out rosy. The Windy City has many fans and is a great baseball town, but my personal living situation (mattress-crashing at unknown houses, then the Y) was strained. The weather was brutal. Barry's time was taken up with social and family engagements. Every bar I went into felt like the proverbial "bar in the wrong neighborhood."

But there was one shining time every day, at 1:00 P.M. when the Cubs game started and Gifford and I were in the press box at Wrigley munching hot dogs with mustard and drinking cold beer. If it rained, my whole day was ruined. The Cubs lost, of course, but that didn't matter. The ambience at Wrigley Field was magic I loved: the gentility of afternoon games, since Wrigley is the only major league ball park still lacking lights.

Wrigley Field, like Bloomington before it, is one of those anachronisms that just can't last, unfortunately. Now that the Cubs have been bought by the *Chicago*

58

Tribune, it seems only a matter of time until lights are installed, and there are persistent rumors of moving the Cubs to a multipurpose indoor dome. It'll be a sad day. Old Man Wrigley, the chewing gum king, never tolerated any change in the place. But new ownership has already spruced up the park some, leaving the ivy and red-brick walls, of course, but applying paint and trying to build a new image for the team. They got so silly they actually changed the Cubs' logo of a smiling Cubbie bear to a growling, angry-looking Cubbie bear. But Cubbie bears are baby bears, they're just plain cute and could never be menacing. The Cubs still lose.

On the north side of town, the White Sox are also under new management and sprucing up their act, but they've become winners, or at least contenders. The Sox were out of town while Gifford and I were in it, so I missed Comiskey Park on that trip, but have been there in the past. It was always a rough-and-tumble, worn-down place with girders and posts and burly, blue-collar fans. Comiskey, remember, was the scene of the Anti-Disco Riot that prevented the second game of a 1979 doubleheader with Detroit because the fans overran the field and set a bonfire of disco records.

The White Sox went from Bill Veeck's consortium (which just didn't have the money to buy star players or fix up the ball park) to new, young, and well-heeled owners who are trying to attract a better game and better class of customer to the North Side. With veterans like Ron LeFlore, Carlton Fisk, Greg Luzinski, Tom Paciorek, and Steve Kemp suddenly with the Chicago club, they figure to be much tougher in the future than they've been in the past.

Peter Gammons, in the *Boston Globe,* has predicted

that Chicago, with both teams undergoing restoration, could well be "*the* baseball town of the eighties." It's certainly a good town for baseball, if not for me.

My own time there ended at two o'clock one morning in front of the downtown Western Union office. I'd had a Seattle friend wire me the money he owed on the purchase of my Montana Jeep for his fish market, and having picked up the cash, was on my way to the airport. Then a very big, very drunk mugger appeared, looming over me like the angel of death and demanding the money I needed to escape. He swung his meaty fist at my head, I ducked and ran like hell. Two blocks away, at the Greyhound depot, I found there was a bus leaving for Boston in fifteen minutes, and made damn sure I was on it.

15

Since baseball time is measured only in outs, all you have to do is succeed utterly; keep hitting, keep the rally alive, and you have defeated time. You remain forever young.

—Roger Angell, in "The Interior Stadium"

For the final month of the 1980 season, I used New York as a base while running to Eastern stadia I'd missed, places like Baltimore and Philadelphia, Atlanta and St. Louis; also Houston. That I don't have a great deal to say about these cities is simply reflective of the fact that I didn't find time or money to stay very long. Still, a brief rundown seems in order.

The Baltimore Orioles has always seemed an admirable organization to me; with its homegrown talent out of the farm system, the team manages to be solidly in contention year after year in a city where attendance and money aren't especially good and the ravages of urban decay have left the ball park a little down on its heels.

The Atlanta Braves are a "TV team" more than any other, since their owner, the outrageous Ted Turner, also owns a cable network that stretches nationwide,

61

and 150 Braves games a year can be seen in homes from Seattle to Bath, Maine. It's little wonder that so few people bother to come out in the heat to the bandbox called County Stadium. Home runs fly out of that place, but unfortunately for the Braves, many of them are off opposing batters' sticks. The battles between Ted and his players over money or position are the most enjoyable ones in baseball. The pitching needs help, but every year the Braves seem a little better. They could make it in this decade, but I somehow doubt that they'll be "America's national team" as Turner likes to predict. They opened the 1982 campaign with a thirteen-game winning streak, that was seen on an estimated 30 million home TV screens. They had come up with such dangerous hit-men as Dale Murphy, Bob Horner, and Chris Chambliss, and best of all, they had found a priceless supporting cast: a mad monk, Brother Francis, who leads cheers on the dugout roof; an ageless wonder, Phil Niekro, who strikes guys out with a maddeningly slow knuckleball; a marble-mouthed rookie out of Methuen, Massachusetts, Steve Bedrosian or "Bedrock"; and that actor-cum-pitcher Al Hrabosky, "The Mad Hungarian," who huffs and puffs and talks to the ball.

The St. Louis Cardinals may be the most improved franchise in baseball, but they're still a team, like the city itself, that I can't get a "feel" for. Like Atlanta, St. Louis gets intolerably hot and humid in the summer, and the weather's been blamed in the past for the team's annual swan dive. But good trades (Ozzie Smith, Bruce Sutter) and smart managing (Whitey Herzog) have given the Cards a real chance. The Cardinals had the best record in the National League East by 1981, despite being eliminated by the bizarre split-season standings. Watch for the Cards and Expos to dominate that division in the future.

At the Astrodome in Houston it's science-fiction ball all the way. There's something spooky about baseball played indoors, no sun or wind, under artificial lights like you were in a theater or something. It's enough to give you a rash.

The Astro organization nonetheless has done very well tailoring this team to the dimensions and problems of the Dome. Since homers are very rare, they go for good pitching, tight defense, and speed on the base paths. The Astros beat you by a run, but they beat you.

September 1980 found the Houston Astros and Los Angeles Dodgers in such close proximity on the charts that they finished the season in a tie and had to play the extra playoff game on a brilliant Monday in October. I watched the game on TV in Gloucester, Massachusetts, with my brother's family. The Astros won, 9–2, striking great joy in the house as we were none of us Dodger fans.

Beating the Dodgers put Houston into a five-game pennant playoff with the Philadelphia Phillies—a playoff that many later said was the finest such series ever. The last four of the five games all went into extra innings, while my brother and I pounded each other on the back.

We had a joke about Houston's center fielder, Terry Puhl. "He's a *Puhl* hitter!" Every time Puhl came up, it seemed, he bashed a line drive base hit to drive in the crucial run. In the fifth game, with Houston leading 5–2 in the top of the ninth, the Phillies came up with five runs to take a 7–5 lead. We'd had the victory in our pockets for a moment, only to see it slip away. We sat in stunned disbelief. "How many did they get?" my brother asked, repeatedly, dazed. He knew all too well. "Five, they got five," I sighed. I can still hear myself.

But the Astros came back in their half of the ninth with two to tie it, 7–7, and we went wild again. It was the culmination of five extremely exciting, strategic ball games, and the winner would go to the World Series. Houston'd made it on great hitting by Puhl, Jose Cruz, and Joe Morgan, and even greater pitching by their killer rotation (Nolan Ryan, Joe Niekro, Bob Knepper, and, of course, Don Sutton). And they'd taken good advantage of the science-fiction atmosphere of the Astrodome.

In the end however, the Phillies emerged victorious in ten, thanks to Mike Schmidt, and earned their ticket to the Fall Classic. I was disappointed but set my sights on the City of Brotherly Love.

Meanwhile, the Kansas City Royals were pounding the Yankees out of the pennant in three straight, with George Brett's three-run homer off Gossage the *pièce de résistance*. Compared to the Houston-Philly series, the New York–Kansas City one was a dull affair: For example, in the Houston-Philly series, the Astros were forever forced to make a decision whether to let their punchless pitcher bat for himself, or go to the bench for a pinch-hitter who might be batting only .200. They made a few runs by having the pitcher sacrifice himself to advance the runner. They also had the luxury of giving intentional walks to opposing batters, in order to get to the pitcher. None of this strategy exists in the American League, since the designated hitter rule was invented by

Charlie Finley, who's my candidate for the single person who's done the worst for baseball in its history. The Royals were euphoric about finally beating the Yanks, but that triumph must have taken everything they had in them. In the World Series that followed, they were tired and ineffective.

16

War is hell.

—William Tecumseh Sherman

Nineteen-eighty was the last season before Ronald Reagan. Throughout that year United States hostages were being held in Iran and war was in the air. Something called the Moral Majority reared its ugly head, neither moral nor any majority. A heat wave killed hundreds of people in Texas and the Southwest, inflation soared. The movie of the year was *Ordinary People*, about some very extraordinary people with *tsuris* you wouldn't believe. The auto industry went nearly banko. The original cast of "Saturday Night Live" resigned to be replaced by an ersatz crew without humor. Bob Dylan became a born-again Christian.

It wasn't the best of years, or the most hopeful advent of a new decade. While the government tried to throw up more and more dangerous nuclear power plants, people stomped to rock music at the No Nukes concerts in Madison Square Garden and protestors flooded the gates of Seabrook, Diablo, Three Mile Island. Draft registration was reinstated. Abortion suddenly became an issue again.

I was scared to death. Looking out over Christopher Street toward the Hudson, I could see the end of it, the Second Coming, if you will, the holocaust. Even the baseball turned mean while the leaves turned brown. The turning point of the World Series occurred in Kansas City in the fifth game, when a rookie Philadelphia pitcher named Dickie Noles issued a ball that came *this* close to nailing George Brett squarely in the head. Beanballs can never be proved to be intentional, but everybody in baseball knows about the purpose-pitch, and there was no mistaking that one. Brett hit the dirt, came up shaken, and didn't hit in the Series thereafter. Nor did many of his fellow Royals. All I could think was "Rick, Rich, Dick, Richie, yes I could understand, but *Dickie?*"

Kansas City was the only city to deny me press credentials, so I got to not go there. Philadelphia, on the other hand, is so close to New York that we could drive from the corner of Christopher and Bleecker in the Village to the ball park in two hours, and drive home that night. Ah, but there was a definite "mean" edge to the Phil's town. They were famous for bickering and bitching among themselves, for not cooperating with the press (except for the affable Tug McGraw), for consorting with odd prescriptions. Ever notice how their certain ace pitcher sniffles and twitches his nose between pitches? Ever ride the El out to the universe of broken glass and brick tenements? Ever eat scrapple at dawn in some dive?

As a kid, I fancied it would be a great thing indeed, a wondrous thing, to be sitting in person at a World Series game, cheering for my team, participating in that fine madness and annual fever. What I hadn't counted upon was the fact that if your own team isn't playing, if in fact you are sitting in the enemy's camp, the cheers are not your own and actually hurt and the World Series can be as anxious and painful as delightful.

I'd filed my papers in person with the Commissioner of Baseball's office in Rockefeller Center, by St. Patrick's Cathedral, and even stopped in there to admire the arches. St. Pat's, that is, not Bowie Kuhn's. When I got my "credentials," I went down with my friend John in some old car. The second game of the series had been a rousing Philadelphia victory—so much so I had actually feared that the mezzanine press box would collapse under the thunderous foot-stomping cheering. "If it's made in Philadelphia, it might be faulty," I reasoned. (Although I'd once fallen in love in the City of Brotherly Love and it was divine. We stayed in an apartment across from the Philadelphia Museum of Fine Art and didn't come out for three days. "If it could happen in Philadelphia," I thought, "it could happen anywhere; and if it could happen to me, it could happen to anybody!")

17

These are the saddest of possible words:
    "Tinker to Evers to Chance."
Trio of bear cubs and fleeter than birds,
    "Tinker to Evers to Chance."
Ruthlessly pricking our gonfalon bubble,
Making a Giant hit into a double—
Words that are heavy with nothing but trouble:
    "Tinker to Evers to Chance."
                              —Franklin P. Adams

The fall of 1980 came right on schedule, with cold nights and early darkness and the sure feeling that the End is near—not only in the baseball season.

Some very threatening words were flying around the country. Without baseball to distract and amuse, how would the winter go? Would there be spring, and spring training? Whatever notions I had of remaining in the East were diminished daily as the cold weather set in. One freezing night in Newburyport, I thought my bones had gone dead and my blood frozen solid. It's one thing to go to a warm climate in the winter for a vacation; it's quite another to realize that you can't withstand the winter, you have no choice, that like some bird you have to fly to the warm or die.

By the middle of November, with the full realization that it was already too late to drive across the country, I headed west from New York in another of my two-hundred-dollar cars, suddenly hungry to quit the road and make a home of some kind, close to my kid out West. I was crazed with fear and worry for the country, fairly unsure of economic survival, and even taking a dreadful chance of breaking down in Minnesota and being lost forever in a midwestern snowscape, but New York and the season and all the mad traveling (four times cross-country) had left me exhausted and fixing to die. I knew a good place to do it.

The car never did get past Minneapolis—once again, of course—but I was able to get enough money for it to finish my trip by Amtrak. Staring out the window of the club car, I saw Montana whipped by snow and wind, and felt so glad to be safe and warm and not driving. Thanksgiving found me back in wet Seattle, eating turkey dinner with my son in some restaurant and lodged in a highway motel by the week, grateful just to be alive.

TWO

Seasons
of Discontent

18

---

from all sides beyond, songs
of invisible birds;
behind my head, through screen,
the kettle boils.
further within, faintly,
the Red Sox trail, 3–2,
while through moist air, miles away,
a truck shifts down, climbing.
                    —Richard Coutant,
          "layers of sound: Fisch Farm"

I have never been able to accept that the season has ended. After the 1979 World Series, won in thrilling fashion by the Pittsburgh Pirates with old Pops Stargell ablaze and an impossibly skinny side-armer, Kent Tekulve, in the bullpen, I flew to Japan to watch the U.S. National and American League All-Stars compete with each other and several Japanese teams. It was a way to keep the game in my life. I planned to get back by Christmas, which means a lot to the children in my life. But things went awry, comically at first, then more seriously. I underestimated the colossal impact of Japan itself on my consciousness. I just couldn't get out of there until after Christmas, after the funeral of a friend of mine, after my heart had been shattered by Japanese eyes.

But the first days had to do with nothing more than clothing: The seamstress who made our Writers' Baseball Association shoulder patches had declared that she could not have them ready until December 26—and when you leave a sewing order with an old lady in Yokosuka, you are honor bound to pick it up.

In Japan, "Chrees-masu" is of course an adopted holiday. So, appropriately, it is recast as a cross between Halloween and New Year's Eve. Santa Claus in the department store is usually female, and at office parties she is often nude. Riotously drunken employees must display their "hidden talents," which amount to singing and dancing around in crazy costumes. The *Chrees-masu pah-tay* is a full-scale national institution by now. Shopping districts have gaudy and dazzling Xmas displays, which disappear completely on the day after the event.

I was invited to a *Chrees-masu pah-tay* staged by friends in the small resort town of H——. We started the day with a shopping expedition to Kamakura, and I was advised to purchase only one gift, and given a modest price limit. The gifts were to be exchanged on a random basis, so the item had to be equally suited to either sex. I asked a friend what kind of gift I should purchase and he said, "Buy vegetables. Vegetables are expensive and everybody would enjoy some." But I *couldn't* buy vegetables for a Christmas present . . . ah, no. After wandering through many shops, utterly lost, I spotted some gourmet coffee from Colombia in tins. All of my friends in Japan drink coffee, it can cost three or four dollars a cup in the cafés, and it's more romantic than vegetables. I bought a pound of the Colombian and gift-wrapped it with a bow.

74

Meanwhile, the elves began laying in liquor for the *pah-tay*. As a special treat, they got sweet, carbonated strawberry wines from San Francisco. The United States price of $1.49 a bottle was still affixed, but they paid ten bucks apiece. Then there was the inevitable *Chrees-masu kay-ki* with gooey white frosting and a cartoon Santa Claus icing, thick and sugary. Next came oceans of wine punch, orangey stuff with floating strawberries. Some bottles of *sake*. And, I noted with joy, plenty of *sushi*, *sashimi*, and other traditional Japanese foods. I wondered who was paying for the feast.

When Christmas night fell, and it was time to go to the *pah-tay*, my translator objected that I had not put on my costume. You have to wear a silly costume at *Chrees-masu*. And the men have to do their own makeup— lipstick, rouge, eye shadow. My translator turned into an outer-space person swathed in crinkly aluminum foil and topped with crazy antennae, and carried a bottle of disappearing ink to splash on startled guests; I turned into a transvestite baseball player. With my Giants cap and jacket, female face, and crazy green swimming trunks pulled over orange long johns, I was the "srender shortstop." The fun had begun. I'd always had a yen to go in drag, but never expected to find a social context in which it was *de rigueur*. We crammed four very weird-looking people in a small car, and made it on over to the bash.

At the formerly staid veterinarian's home, the whole village of H—— had turned into giraffes, gypsy ladies, and clowns. The stereo blared disco hits from the States, the favorite hymn being "YMCA" by the Village People, which I had thought was played only in gay bars. The Japanese treat it as an English lesson, and form the letters *Y, M, C, A* with their bodies as they leap around on the dance floor. Think I'll have some more orangey punch. Flashing green and red lights formed zigzag patterns of loony light. That punch isn't so bad after all; tastes like Kool-Aid but it gets you smashed. Getting smashed is old Chrees-masu tradition. The room swam before me as practical jokers played outrageous tricks and people stood to sing or recite.

When it was announced time to open the *presentos*, all the guests formed a circle on the floor and each was issued a number by some meticulous process that assured one could not receive the presento he had brought. The numbers were called off, and each presento opened to roars of drunken laughter. The first gift was a rubber statue of a muscleman who, when his arms were lifted, pissed. An orange tank-top shirt with lurid blue script, "Surfin' California." A savings bank in which the bony arm of a corpse comes out of a coffin and snatches the coin. I sat in mute horror. Why hadn't the friend who advised me to buy vegetables told me that Chrees-masu was a joke? I knew whoever got the coffee was going to be disappointed.

The person who received the gift had to identify the giver, and the crowd chanted "Who? Who? Who?" until he or she guessed right. Then, the giver had to give the receiver a kiss. In the case of two men, the receiving man pretends to be a woman to the vast amusement of all. Light bulbs went on in my head. So that's why the guys need makeup. Finally, the dreaded thing happened: The woman next to me opened the coffee presento.

The room fell into total silence for half a minute. The woman kept turning the can upside down, staring at it in disbelief and saying *"Kohi desu-ka?"* Is it really coffee? My crimson mortification was an unnecessary clue to my guilt, for everybody knew that only the *gaijin* would have bought something practical for a Chrees-masu presento. I dispensed with the kiss quickly, and the pah-tay carried on. I received a crazy paperweight with a cartoon naked couple inside. I apologized to my host for being just a Catholic boy from Massachusetts who never experienced Chrees-masu before.

There followed other games: All guests kneel in a circle and bow until their heads touch the floor. At that moment, one person gets whacked over the head with a rolled-up newspaper and has to guess the identity of his assailant, then give him or her a kiss. There was a lot of public kissing and giggling. I was glad when the food was served and we all ate oceans of raw fish and other delicacies, then the pah-tay was declared over and everybody went home happy and drunk. (In Japan, it is not a crime to drive when drunk; indeed, if you have an accident, the assumption is it's not your fault *because* you were drunk.) The host stood at the door collecting a precise sum of money from each guest for his share of the food expenses. I handed in my four thousand yen thinking, "Chrees-masu in Japan: The things I do for baseball."

19

Although violence is forbidden by the Code, occasionally tempers flare and things get out of hand. When this happens, Japanese players will lash out with an intensity seldom seen in American ball parks.

—Robert Whiting, in *The Chrysanthemum and the Bat*

I have mentioned that I was waiting for a seamstress to deliver Writers' Baseball Association patches. She came through on schedule, but rearranged the words in classic Japanese fashion, putting the last name first: "Association Writers' Baseball." But I have to point out that neither the WBA nor the AWB is associated with the Baseball Writers Association of America. The latter organization is exclusive to those gentlemen and a few ladies who cover baseball as a full-time occupation for established newspapers; the WBA is a group of writers who happen to be addicted to baseball. Our sole function is to hang around at ball parks, where we get stoned, drinking beer and analyzing the game. We have our letterhead, matching envelopes, press cards, and shoulder patches. We proudly boast offices in Boston, New York, Chicago, and San Francisco, but we have no address or phone number.

The whole thing started in the box seats on the first-base side at the Oakland Coliseum, where the A's were playing the Red Sox in a night game. It was in the dark age when Charlie Finley owned the team despite many attempts to unload it, and, typically, there was some foul-up with the tickets. Instead of being in the mob of red-capped Sox fans along the third-base line, we were thirty rows up among the local yahoos. Tom Farber was enraged. Tom is a short-story writer with a lifelong umbilical attachment to the Bostons. Red Sox fans thrive on aggravation. We had a splendid time anyway, and Barry Gifford, the writer who belongs to the Chicago Cubs, suggested that we needed a *club*, that with our pal Gerald Rosen, also a novelist, holding down the Giants, we were already an association that met regularly with the highest of professional conferences. "It's too bad there's already a Baseball Writers Association," I said. "We can be the Writers' Baseball Association," Farber laughed, "and any confusion will only be to our benefit!"

Well, of course the WBA spread across the literary baseball community like wildfire. We were swamped with applications for membership from writers around the world who value the prestigious WBA credentials and ballot in the WBA Awards. Our awards don't fit into set categories like the Cy Young or Most Valuable Player awards, but recognize individual achievements—Bonehead Play of the Week, Most Sexually Attractive Player, etc., etc.

I was, at any rate, in Japan on a WBA mission, that of forming our Japanese affiliate, the JWBA. Japan is nuts about baseball, it's played everywhere and on TV every night. But the rules are a little different; for one thing, it's considered terribly rude to argue with the umpire, and U.S. players have to quash their natural aggression toward umpires if they expect to play in Japan. I mean, the umpire's the man, he gets respect. If the pitcher hits the batter, he has to tip his cap in apology. Should he fail to tip his cap, which is rare, the opposing team is entitled to plunk a guy their next time up. Nowhere is this rule written down, but Japanese fans and players all know it.

Like employees of large corporations (which in fact they are—most of the teams are owned by major industry), Japanese baseball players tend to be loyal, are rarely traded and sold as in the United States, and never quarrel with ownership about money. The legendary Sadaharu Oh asked for a cut in pay after the '79 season because he hit "only" thirty-nine home runs. The fans cheer and yell, of course, but will be silent at critical moments as a courtesy to the pitcher's concentration. It's like baseball turned inside-out—the same game played in a different spirit.

The spectacle of the U.S. All-Stars in Japan was marred by more than a few breaches of politeness. The general idea was that the best stars from both leagues in the United States would play the best of the Japanese leagues in a series of post-season exhibition contests. The U.S. players were promised, or led to believe, they had a good crack at signing lucrative endorsement contracts with Japanese industries. The players felt underpaid at about five thousand dollars per man (for seven games over two weeks' time). Then the promised endorsements didn't materialize except, from what I can tell, for Pete Rose.

In '81 Rose was publicly flacking a Japanese bat. Imagine—the wood for the stick that broke Stan Musial's National League hit record was probably grown in western Canada or the Pacific Northwest, shipped to Japan, and then shipped back to Pete Rose in Philly. Rose was essentially working for the Japanese, who more and more are competing with traditional U.S. firms like Rawlings and Wilson for the ball, glove, and bat markets. The SSK Corporation, for instance, makes the new "dimpled" fielder's glove, which is a substantial improvement on the American glove since it "grips" the ball tighter. Japanese manufacturers now set up sales trailers at the spring training camps in Arizona and Florida and sell their products to the big-leaguers, and if you think they've surpassed us in the automotive and electronic and computer and nuclear fields, just wait and see what they're going to do to baseball in the next decade!

The U.S. All-Stars were more than aware of the potential for big bucks working for the Japanese baseball industry, or industries. When the players didn't get the endorsement contracts, a number of them stalked out of the series. Their wives complained of the high cost of shopping in Tokyo, and some players were actually rude enough to bitch about raw fish. Add to that the fact that big, tall guys have a rough time finding comfortable furniture and beds in Japan, or clothing in the right sizes.

The players were rude to their Japanese hosts, and rudeness is the one thing that is most unforgivable in Japan. It is also the heart and soul of baseball in America. There is nothing dignified about a ninety-seven-mph spheroid flying squarely toward your heart. Such a rock-hard missile could knock your eye out, and you better believe that the hitters know it. I've had sharp line-drive foul balls whiz past my ear in the stands or the press box, and knew the fear of God. In Japan, the game is more sedate, even if real life isn't.

You think a D train from West 4th Street to Columbus Circle at rush hour is unendurable because you're scrunched and can't breathe? Such a New York subway ride would seem painless and commodious in Tokyo, where you can actually suffer broken bones from the pressure of other human bodies against your own, and actually die from breathing in a "bad air pocket." Environmental pollution and the steady elimination of open space and natural resources have advanced to the point where some citizens indulge in *organized rudeness* to protest the fact that Japan is committing national suicide. You've seen the newspaper photos of Japanese students in crash helmets, carrying sticks and battling the cops. In fighting against U.S. nuclear weapons in Japan, the new Tokyo Narita airport, or the government's plan to place nuclear power plants up and down the earthquake-prone Honshu coast, these *samurai* are fighting not only for their lives, but possibly also ours.

Some dear friends, long involved in the Narita airport protest, invited me to a demonstration. They knew that I'd been politically active in the States and probably didn't know that it'd been years since I went to a demonstration. There was no way to politely refuse, so I traveled with them the two hours on crowded trains out to the Narita airport, for which the government usurped the lands of many farming families. The airport is thus symbolic of the eventual doom.

My hosts had described the Narita demonstration as something of a civilized affair. I had no idea that I was riding into one of the most purely terrifying experiences you could imagine. Hanging by a strap in the subway heading toward Narita, I read for the first time (in that day's English-language *Japan Times*) that the demonstration was to be met by two thousand armed soldiers, that numbers of people had died in the act of resisting, that arrests and casualties were common. I would have hopped off and grabbed the first train back to town except for feeling committed to my friends.

We finally arrived in a small town and boarded special buses for the airport site. I was surrounded by people, mostly young, dressed in battle attire. My apprehension reached the level of acute paranoia when our bus stopped and heavily armed police searched the passengers. As I was sitting at the back of the bus, I had a moment in which to stuff my joints into my underwear, where they fortunately escaped detection. But I could feel my heart pounding and imagined I must be blushing. Possession of marijuana is a serious crime in Japan; hell, they kept Paul McCartney in a solitary cell on bread and coffee for two weeks for being foolish enough to throw six ounces of reefer in his suitcase. Somebody should have explained to Paul that you have to carry it in on your person; they won't touch your person, they don't even shake hands, but bow.

(In one paragraph, I've been body-searched *and* assured you that Customs will never touch your body, and if that seems a contradiction, it is. Put simply: The Narita demonstration was a departure from Japanese *form*, a kind of war game, in which the normal rules of politeness were abandoned and a free-for-all ensued. Imagine that your whole life is constricted by rigid codes of behavior and protocol, and you are suddenly in one of the two exceptional situations—war and sex—in which you are free to go mad.)

The protestors' camp was like some D. W. Griffith movie on the front lines of World War I. Bonfires filled the air with blue smoke. Helmeted leaders screamed into microphones, and squad marshals herded their troops around with bullhorns. Banners and placards were everywhere, of course, and my hosts explained to me the various neat clusters of radicals: the blue-helmeted Marxists, the white-helmeted Anarchists, the red-helmeted Communists, etc. Drumbeats rumbled. Just on the edge of the camp, armies of blue, stoic guardians of the peace marched and raced down the streets in snakelike processions. Their arms: caustic tear gas, smoke bombs, bullets if necessary. I lost my friends in the melee, and latched on to a Dutch magazine photographer who spoke some English and gave me the best advice yet—he taught me the Japanese word for "newspaper reporter" and advised me to scream it like bloody murder when the cops advanced.

Now, I'm opposed to the Narita airport as much as to the San Francisco airport and all airports. I'm opposed to nuclear power. I want to live to be 102. But my disapproval of the land-ravaging Narita development and the whole direction of nuclear madness in Japan ran squarely up against my natural desire to escape harm, stay alive, and hold on to my pot. It seemed a difficult proposition, but I decided to try to cross the police lines and get to safety.

Walking away from the demonstration, I must have passed hundreds of frantically active cops who totally ignored me. Finally I reached a small restaurant that had no customers but was open. The elderly couple who ran the place evidently lived in the back room. I sat cross-legged at the table, directly facing a picture window where I had a ringside view of the action. Tanks, fleeing students, six hundred arrested, forty wounded, no fatalities. The tiny old woman kept refilling my *sake* glass to the brim, and her husband brought me rice and vegetables, *gyoza* and Kirin beers. I sat there for three or four hours, shaken by the realization that I'm too old to fight in the streets anymore.

20

Fanaticism? No. Writing is exciting and baseball is like writing.

—Marianne Moore, from "Baseball and Writing"

Ron had the shack in Seattle's Ballard district simply for the purpose of tearing it down, but with all the new laws and zoning and building permits and other bureaucratic stuff involved, he found himself with less than enough money to destroy the house. The shack itself was worth less than nothing, but the hill it stood on commanded a 180-degree view of the city, Puget Sound, and the Olympic Mountains to the West. Sunsets were religiously inspiring. The house was valued at $1.00 and the lot at $100,000.

The front door of the house had been shattered throughout when the previous tenant hurled his body through it at the end of an especially noisy Halloween party. Indeed, destroying the house had been part of the entertainment of the evening. It was assumed that no human person would ever live there again. It was unforeseeable that I'd blow into town from my travels, with an ex-Marine I'd picked up hitchhiking, and find

86

Seattle closed to casual renters. The vacancy rate was under one percent and prices were triple what they'd been only five years earlier. The demon that is driving Seattle in its latest boom cycle is aerospace industry and the military. "We're floating into the eighties on war money, it's the war that's making Seattle rich," smiled David Brewster, editor of *The Weekly.*

The ex-Marine reminded me of Carl, an earlier fellow traveler. I guess I first met Carl on that hopeless Chinese freighter between Singapore and Hong Kong. Come to think of it, the freighter wasn't too different from the Seattle shack. Both had leaky roofs, and both required walking outside to get to the indoor bathroom. Carl was downstairs on the lower deck eating white rice, bland vegetables, and stringy meat with the mostly Chinese second-class passengers. Other Americans riding second class on this particular boat would be young, as I was at the time, but Carl was in late middle age. His drooping mustache was nearly grayed over, his angular face charted with rivers of worry and laughter. We joked about the poor quality of the food while our Chinese friends enjoyed their family dinner; then we headed for the bar, a never-ending card game, and conversation that unraveled our emotional lives in the calm of the South China Sea.

Carl had been a professor of sociology at Harvard. He had a wife, though they'd started living apart, and a daughter and son full-grown. He got a small check every month from a real-estate investment, enough to keep moving around Asia, riding third-class trains and staying in boardinghouse arrangements with local people. It was possible to live comfortably there for $200 a month plus travel costs.

Carl's high forehead suggested thoughtfulness, and he came up with clear analyses of situations I had thought exotic and mysterious. He reduced the cultures of Asia to commonsense Bostonian judgments. Of the Japanese he'd say, "They try to kill you with kindness, but they don't know how to take a joke." Of the Indians, "They still eat with their hands." My generation of Eastern traveler was perhaps too sincerely in search of gurus and spiritual enlightenment (or dope or commerce) to admit to the deficiencies in life we all suffered. As Americans, we were accustomed to living standards unknown to the Far East. We had never before (or since) lived in such filth, with so poor a diet and such run-of-the-mill problems as diarrhea, infection, and discomfort. Still, our adulation of "the people" may have brought us closer to them than Carl's disdain. Nonetheless, his maturity and matter-of-fact attitude provided an apt foil for the otherwise dreamy consciousness I'd carried with me from India. If Carl had escaped even the high Himalayas without so much as one dream, I thought, he couldn't continue traveling as he did. It wasn't a comfortable enough life for a sociologist to endure, unless he was running away from a bad situation at home. While his words were usually irreverent and to the point, Carl's silences were awesomely significant. The missing element in his stories was his wife, of whom he spoke distantly but gave little information. I felt all my failed romances spilling over the deck and overboard without restraint. We drank bottle after bottle of duty-free Johnnie Walker Red. I had given up searching for my guru after a year of ups and downs; Carl had never imagined even bothering with such an idea. We took a cabin together.

We were the only Americans on the boat, though there was a party of Australians who rode first class, kept to themselves, and shouted "Bloody inconsiderate!" and so forth every time the Chinese servants or crew got in their way. They were formally polite to us, but obviously viewed us as degenerates and didn't court our company. Carl and I had both planned on visiting Australia when we left the United States, but abandoned the idea after meeting the general drift of travelers from Darwin, Sydney, and Melbourne. Singapore, behind us, had been a disappointment after the wildness of India and Indonesia; Singapore, more than any Asian city outside of Japan and mainland China, had "tightened up." I had had to tie my longish hair into a ponytail and carefully hide it under the stiff collar of a Western shirt I'd bought in Madras expressly for that purpose. Visas were denied to long-haired men. By comparison, I did and could travel around India and Nepal in a state of dishevelment equaled only by the untouchables, with my loose clothing and long hair flying in the hot monsoon winds. I was not trying to affect a state of dissipation for any romantic reasons: The light khotas and dhotis were simply the only comfortable gear in the beastly midsummer heat. It took daily dousing with cream rinse to untangle the knots in my hair. I was, for the first time, solely responsible for taking care of myself.

We were men alone on the road. My marriage and children and subsequent pain in separation and divorce were all to come, his were past. Perhaps someday, I thought, I'd be like Carl: my children grown, I'd retrace my steps across Asia and be a single man who can, somehow, stand alone and all together—as Carl did. Asked why he chose to travel professionally, he said,

"There was no reason *not* to." He was no more *lacking* a family and employment than an arm or leg. He was, I was, a little universe on the South China Sea. Nobody needed us back home, and we couldn't allow ourselves to need each other. At each port, one makes the decision where to go next. Men traveling casually might become good friends, even lending money and sharing their worldly estates, but they seldom made the more serious commitment of understanding each other. How to love somebody you know you won't see again?

No, it's a kind of camaraderie that doesn't heal the basic loneliness in any of us but fills our hours with pleasant, pointless conversation and smoke, drink, music perhaps, games of all sorts. Men at play seem like men at work sometimes.

21

There was ease in Casey's manner as he stepped
into his place.
There was pride in Casey's bearing and a smile
lit Casey's face . . .
—Ernest Lawrence Thayer,
from "Casey at the Bat"

Bill, my ex-Marine roommate, was equally cut adrift
from everything in life at the tender age of twenty-one.
He had neither great skill nor adequate education, and
had been taken out of his mother's home and in and out of
institutions since he was seven years old. The Marines
offered him the only alternative to juvenile detention
home, and gave him the best life he'd ever known.
"Plenty a' meat an' potatas, y'know, plenty a' guys to
talk to, jeez, I really loved the Marines. Wish they'd a
take me back, y'know." Bill did something to earn a
dishonorable discharge, but he wouldn't tell me what it
was. He did steal a lot, shoplifting I mean, and not
always intelligently. He'd done time in Oregon, y'know.
He talked constantly about jobs he'd never apply for—
Bill wasn't going to be some fast-food grillman, hell no,
he was a' going to get a real good job, something like a
truck driver's. Except he didn't have a license. Or a

birth certificate. Or a passport. He didn't know where he was born, but he knew he was a Virgo.

Bill's only means of support was his body, which was tall and perfectly muscled, "a *great* body!" he'd say with a boyish grin. He was sure thousands of women would pay him to fuck them, like pathetic Joe Buck in *Midnight Cowboy*, but he had earned his living trading on the affections of older men. That didn't make him gay, though. His neatly kept pile of *Playboy* magazines attested to that, he said. He carried the heavy *Playboy* magazines all over the West. He even "lived in New York" once. Where in New York? "At the Port Authority Bus Station." Business good? "Nah, that place stinks."

Bill's was a soul crying out for "exceptance," as he spelled it. He was glad to sit for hours composing raging verse: Life is unfair! I just need to be excepted by somebody, excepted for whom I am! And he was. Excepted by employers, schools, the welfare office, excepted by his mother and father, friendless, alone, a small child lost on the streets of the capital, maybe never to be somebody to anybody.

The drizzle fell on the seascape of Seattle. The little woodstove was not only the sole heat in the house, but also the source of hot water from the tap. The one room was ventilated where the walls had been stripped of their shingles for kindling. A broken window was patched over with cardboard. The bathtub was in the "kitchen," with a partition providing a small modicum of privacy. My writing desk was an old tabletop propped on two sawhorses, and tilted at a perilous angle so that pencils rolled off like logs and I got a crick in my neck after an hour of sitting there.

We were like George and Lenny in *Of Mice and Men*, a

92

couple of hoboes keeping an old shack warm and digging around for cash for tomorrow's cigarettes and pint. I started going to A.A. meetings. Still it rained every day and baseball seemed gone forever, too distant to recall.

I left town alone for Christmas in California. The Grey Rabbit bus costs only forty dollars from Seattle to Berkeley, an overnight adventure on a 1950 GMC bus converted to sleeping quarters for forty. When you board the Rabbit, you get the spiel: No smoking *tobacco* allowed. Alcohol and food are allowed if shared. Soon, whole picnics come out. Soon your palm's being read, your chart analyzed, and who knows what. For the modern traveler, the Grey Rabbit can't be beat. You can even take it from New York to San Francisco, but beware; the Rabbit has been known to stop for hours at national parks and make three-hundred-mile detours to see some canyon.

I left Bill with a job of some kind—washing dishes in a hotel downtown—and a few bucks, a few logs for the fire, and unrestricted access to the shack until they came to tear it down. He disappeared shortly, and wasn't heard from again for a year, when he turned up one morning fresh from a farm-laboring job in Minnesota.

He'd moved in with his boss on the hotel job, Bill said, to get out of the shack, which had since been flattened. "But the guy got a little pushy, y'know."

22

You have to be a man to be a big leaguer, but you
have to have a lot of little boy in you, too.
                                    —Roy Campanella

What do *you* do in the off-season? Sit around Seattle
and drink? On December 8, 1980, with the full darkness
of no-ball sitting on the cold nation, some crazy guy shot
and killed John Lennon outside the Dakota Apartments
in New York City. Who could believe *that?* We can
understand presidents getting shot, and yes, even in a
way, the Pope, who is a kind of monarch over a vast
political and financial empire. But John Lennon was an
angel of consciousness, a singer of songs, an artist. Had
we forgotten the power of art? It drove poor Mark David
Chapman out of his mind.

Yoko Ono inspired us with her public forgiveness and
calls for peace in the world. No trace of bitterness
crossed her face. Utterly Japanese in her composure and
bearing, she reminded me of the widow of a Japanese
writer, J. Uekusa, whose funeral I attended in Tokyo.
She bowed to me until her forehead touched the tatami
mat, and I bowed as low. The tops of our heads lightly
brushed each other. There were no tears, but the pealing

of soft temple bells and a jazz trumpeter wailing a long, high note.

There's been one too many funerals lately. The rain lashed the old house in Seattle as we sat in Cathy's kitchen feeding the woodstove, looking at the one yellow rose miraculously clinging to the bush, drinking, oh yes, and thinking on John.

"Mama don't go, Daddy come home!"

"God is a concept by which we measure our pain."

Elin Gilbert came into my life in the Northwest with only a whisper of announcement and soon made herself my chief point of focus. You see, a friend who knew I was struggling with failing eyesight took me to meet Elin, who was the undisputed grand lady of the Bates Method in the West. She was in advanced years—exact age a secret, dear—and had been helping people regain their vision for some thirty years in her pleasant studio facing the waterfront, over a gaudy X-rated downtown Seattle theater.

The Bates Method is a system of exercises to relax the body and mind and improve vision. That is, of course, putting it far too simply. Elin went through three intensive years of training to be a Bates teacher and learned all the subtle skills needed to copy with myopia, astigmatism, and other eye diseases. She was one of the few surviving graduates of the Bates School, carried on by Mrs. Margaret Corbett after the death of its founder, Dr. W. H. Bates of New York.

Aldous Huxley was one of Mrs. Corbett's most grateful pupils (no pun intended), and he wrote his Bates book, *The Art of Seeing*, "to repay a debt of gratitude" to her and to Dr. Bates.

But Elin Gilbert did not improve her students' vision

simply by directing or prescribing exercises such as sunning the eyes, "palming," and "swinging." She had the power to *relax* every bone in your body just by being herself around the room. She'd arrange a flower pot, cross the room on crutches left over from her auto accident ("There! I'll soon be running the hundred-yard dash!"), or suddenly start singing or telling stories of her girlhood in Norway.

"Those were innocent times, dear. Do you know my father was so patient with me he once spoon-fed me for two hours—I was so proud, so stubborn. Imagine, dear, we were taught never to lie, and we were never lied to, either. My mother lived to be ninety-two and cooked dinner the night she died. That's her picture on the wall behind you."

Or: "Did you see the lovely painting one of my pupils made for me?" (An outrageous mandala.) Or: "Noticed my dandelions yet? Fresh-picked!" With Elin, it's always notice this, imagine that, look here, look there, *see?* see!

You suddenly realized you were in the presence of a kind and beautiful old lady who's been in the same room for thirty years, six days a week from nine to five, who knows everything about natural food and health and Montessori and has made some effort to make peace with her God. It wasn't always like this. There were the marriages, the ballet, the life in Europe. That was a long time ago.

Anxiety dissipated around Elin. You immediately saw better. Whatever hardships you brought in from the street rolled off your back and for an instant—an eternity—you were caught in Elin's memory lane. *Anxiety, time, memory* are all key words in Bates therapy. Bates was the first ophthalmologist to claim that vision comes from psychological as well as organic health.

You will see well *effortlessly* if you can just let go and let it come, Elin would say. Once she fell asleep in the middle of a particularly dreamy lesson; perched on her stool, sitting straight up without a chair-back to lean on, Elin snoozed peacefully while I swung my gaze around the room, taking in the eye charts and visual parapher-nalia, the old upright piano, the broken-in couch and familiar floral rug—and *I* fell asleep.

Forty minutes later, Elin snapped to, her eyes pop-ping open. "Oh! It was so still in here I almost fell asleep!" she said with a chuckle. Ah! I thought. It's a rare teacher who can induce a midday siesta in my anxious urban life.

Another time, Elin fell so totally asleep that she sank, by gradual degrees, off her stool to the floor. I rushed over from my place in the pupil's armchair (under the toasty-warm heatlamps) to catch her halfway and lower her to the rug, where she lay in a state of sublime repose. I checked her pulse and breathing, and both were slightly peppier than normal. It was fast approach-ing the end of my hour's lesson time, but I couldn't go off leaving Elin on the floor. The issue was resolved for me by Elin herself, who picked up her head at precisely two o'clock and said, "You'd better go, dear, you'll be late for your next appointment."

"But, Elin, I can't leave you on the floor like this!"

"Don't be ridiculous. It's very good for my posture and circulation to sleep on a firm surface, dear."

Elin's freedom to nap was never confused with any shortage of mental acuity. She was lucid in her diagnosis and clear in her instructions. "Now, dear, you will do me a favor this I hope? Yes! Please look *around the edges* of everything!"

"Worrying about money is bad for your eyes, dear."

"You'll never see better if you don't stop telling lies, dear."

23

> To while away the time I play my solitaire card
> baseball game Lionel and I invented in 1942 when
> we visited Lowell and the pipes froze for Christ-
> mas—the game is between the Pittsburgh Plym-
> ouths (my oldest team, and now barely on top of
> the 2nd division) and the New York Chevvies rising
> from the cellar ignominiously since they were
> world champions last year—I shuffle my deck,
> write out the lineups, and lay out the teams—For
> hundreds of miles around, black night, the lamps of
> Desolation are lit, to a childish sport, but the Void
> is a child too—
>
> —Jack Kerouac, from
> *Desolation Angels*

There is always APBA Baseball for the cold months.
It's a board game not unlike the homemade one Kerouac
describes, but immensely more sophisticated. Using the
APBA system, you can manage all the actual major
league players of the day, and over a period of time, they
will perform almost exactly as they do in real life. In
other words, Pete Rose will hit well but not for power,
and Nolan Ryan will strike out a lot of batters. You, as
manager, can pinch-hit, order a sacrifice, change pitchers, strategize, and create a very realistic tabletop base-

ball game in your own kitchen while the snow piles up outside and the dear pastime itself hibernates and players drink beer and put on weight.

APBA fans are legion. Some play a full 162-game schedule between November and March. They have bumper stickers, T-shirts, *The APBA Journal*, visits to the APBA offices. You have to buy a new set of player cards every year to keep current on the averages and statistics, so the company actually keeps a record of the names and addresses of every person who buys a game. (The original setup costs about twenty-five dollars and ten dollars a year for updated cards.) Corresponding with APBA is like relating to a religious organization or some kind of Kabbalistic lodge. The company warns that it will not reply to certain questions and inquiries and offers this:

"Regardless of what you may infer from the letters, APBA does not stand for anything. It is a trade name registered at the United States Patent Office and may not be used for any other product. Its origin goes back to 1932 when the game was in its formative stages and it is of a sentimental, personal origin that would require lengthy explanation. APBA really has no meaning to anyone but us, but if you are a true APBA fan, you must pronounce it 'App-Bah.' Never, no never, call it 'Ay, Pee, Bee, Ay!'"

24

Baseball is a game played by idiots for morons.
—F. Scott Fitzgerald

We lost the election but won the war that winter. I ran for governor of Washington State on the Constant Party ticket, mostly to protest the policies of our then-Guv, Dixy Lee Ray ("Madame Nuke"). My platform was strictly hedonistic, my slogan "Vote for Ray, Not Dixy." The people of Washington did not, fortunately, sweep me into office, but they did sweep Dixy out. Now, it remains only to figure out how much planetary damage got done during the four years she was in there, madly planning nuclear power installations and going as far afield as China to offer Washington State as a haven for deadly toxic wastes.

Dixy Lee Ray was a spectacle of a governor never to be seen again. Short, round, sixty, female, single, she kept dogs in her office, drove a Jeep, and lived in a camper. She said things like, "A nuclear power plant is infinitely safer than eating, because three hundred people choke to death on food every year." She characterized "the world's most important problem" as "runaway population increase. The only answer for this nation is cessation of its efforts to support the rest of the world. Let Nature take its course. Worst of all is rushing in to save starving populations whose unfortunate lot it has been to suffer such irreparable brain damage from severe malnutrition that its children can never be normal."

"We can no longer talk of unearned 'rights.' We'll have to get back to working for 'rights' to adequate food, housing, education, opportunity, a place in the sun—and not everybody is going to make the grade. I don't see this obsession with the lowest strata of humanity, against all natural biologic experience. We must accept that life is unfair."

Or, the essential Chairman Ray: "The first atomic warhead I saw was like a beautiful piece of sculpture, a work of the highest level of technological skill. It's the point of a spear."

I had found my alter ego. I actually proposed marriage to Dixy Lee Ray. (She can't say now she's never been asked.) I figured she had the money and position I lack, and I had the sense she lacked of caring for a future world for our children to inherit. I was even willing to change my last name so I could be Ray Mungo Ray and she wouldn't have to be Dixy Lee Ray Mungo. The Seattle *Weekly* published my love letters to her. Cold silence from the Executive Mansion.

I liked to think Dixy's decline and eventual rout in the 1980 election was a foretaste of things to come for the current Republican administration, but who knew? Even the KKK was on the march again, and just what were we waiting for?

25

I know winning isn't everything, but with Calvin
Griffith winning isn't anything.
                    —Ron Davis, on being traded
                    from the Yankees to the Twins

Blast off-seasons anyway. Try to keep up with all the
trades and selling of players from one team to the next.
There's no longer such a thing as loyalty to one's team
where millions of bucks are involved. There's even a
strike in the air, and not the kind that comes when you
swing and miss but the kind that comes when you don't
work for your employer. They say "Play ball!" when they
mean "Work ball!" The last thing we need is to see
baseball go down the tubes with the rest of the country.

26

A milk-and-water, goody-goody player can't wear a
Cleveland uniform.

—Patsy Tebeau,
Cleveland manager, 1892

I do a little teaching in the off-season, at the Centrum
Foundation in Jefferson County, state of Washington.

The Centrum Foundation hosts a conference of forty
or fifty high school students who have been chosen by
teachers and a panel of judges to be the best creative
writers in the state high schools. Every year the kids
come to Port Townsend and live in dorms at Fort Wor-
den, an army post turned seaside park, for a week,
attending classes, readings, and individual conferences
with their teachers, who are all professional, working
writers.

And every year the kids smoke pot and drink beer and
go out on the beach after curfew and do other such things
that one expects from healthy American teen-agers.

And every year *some*body gets upset.

We're not talking major delinquency here. This is not some New York City street gang. On the contrary, all of these kids come from middle-class towns, from Yakima, Omak, or Walla Walla, and all are honor students. The ones who truly *burn* to be writers get a chance to be exposed to actual published writers, usually for the first time in their lives. Imagine being sixteen and growing up in Spokane with your nose in a book—escaping, always, the drab reality of a small Northwest city—and suddenly finding yourself in the presence of an author whose books you may have read, *and* away from your parents and tossed in with other precocious kids. It's heady wine for young minds. When *I* was sixteen, the best I could do was write letters to authors, most of whom never answered.

In other words, it's a good idea and a good program. But it is not without its detractors, particularly when the after-curfew hijinks come into play and the foundation's administrators have to placate hysterical mothers, irate legislators, and the local constabulary.

I was one of three faculty members at the conference, as I had been a year earlier. We were housed in a large apartment at the fort, to which our students came for their conferences and occasional evening gatherings.

As it happened, the kids came over to the faculty residence on a Tuesday night, the second evening of the conference, and smoked a little grass and drank some beer—the quantities of both were modest and the quality of the former so poor that nobody got smashed—then left at 10:20 P.M., twenty minutes beyond their dorm curfew. We pushed them out the door with exhortations to get back to the dorm pronto. We had been sitting around discussing books and writing; but as the story circulated around town, it got more colorful. Some said it was a wild party; nobody accused us of improprieties, but rumors flew. In fact, it was an innocent evening.

The students, alas, did not have the good sense to return to their dorms, where they would have been mildly chided for lateness. They went to the beach in the wet, freezing night and sat in a cave with the soles of their feet pressed together for warmth, and recited—*poetry*. That, at least, is the account of one of them, who wrote a story about the experience. He ended the story with the remark that it was worth breaking any rule and suffering any punishment for that moment on the beach.

Some of the kids had taken, at my invitation, copies of a small literary magazine called *Green Mountain Post*, for which I edited an issue. The magazine contains a fiction piece, "Maui Wowee," which the author (Harvey Wasserman) meant as a parody of pornographic literature. Some who read it, though, think it's *really* dirty.

The stage was thus set for the Guns of April.

By Wednesday morning, several hysterical mothers had already arrived to take their children away from the nefarious Writers Conference. While most of the kids were loose, there were a few Christers and very straight kids who blew the whistle on the others. They found all three faculty members offensive, too. We were accused of using foul language both in our work and in our speech, of being blasphemous, of not offering a structured, disciplined class procedure with assignments and grading! The last point was especially galling. Writers who teach these seminars feel that these kids get all the assignments and grading they need from their English teachers at school; what a working writer has to offer is appreciation and criticism, simply being with the young writers and giving them a real picture of what a writer is, how a writer works. This is teaching of an invaluable sort.

We were further accused of keeping our students out after curfew, imbibing illegal substances in their presence, and I was accused of distributing pornography (whatever *that* is, legally speaking) on state property in a state-funded educational program! At this point, the Jefferson County sheriff got involved in some vague and mysterious way. He had been *seen* driving across the grounds early in the day, purportedly investigating the previous night's adventures.

The foundation administrators were left with the unpleasant task of placating irate parents, students, and even some legislators. It was their noble calling to defend the arts and artists against attacks from yahoos and fundamentalists who everywhere populate the state. The way they chose to do it was to force the kids to return their copies of *Green Mountain Post* magazine, and to whisk me off in a Mercedes for the next ferry to Seattle. I stepped off the boat and safely back into King County an hour before the opening of the Mariners' first game.

My students were upset. Some cried. Some dropped out of the program. I got a marvelous chance to deliver heroic parting lines. But they are the ones who got cheated. Having no choice, I left them behind.

Sad ending.

27

When the end of the world comes, Seattle will still
have one more year to go.

> —Dick Vertlieb,
> former Mariner executive

Ye pilgrims all to Kingdome came
For the opening ball of the Mariner
    game.
Many hot dogges were therein ingested.
While the Angels our new, blue, boys
    molested.

But the Halos were tarnished in game
    number three
(Which coincided with Good Friday)
And Ruppert Jones went to hell at bat,
To push us over on Holy Sat.

Now, Mariner fans are all of a feather:
For a moment of victory we'll follow
    forever
Our trident team as it comes to pass,
On sunless diamond, and vinyl grass.

THREE

The Season
Canceled
Due to Rain

28

No other sport can match baseball's flair for the appropriate. The last news of the 1981 season, by all odds the worst in the history of the pastime, was made away from the field by a nonparticipant in the games, and it simultaneously demeaned the players and insulted the fans. Perfect.

—Roger Angell, in
The New Yorker

I was talking with my friend Marco about the upcoming Mariner season as the train pulled slowly through the Rockies, bound for Seattle. Marco's an Amtrak porter so he gets a free ride down to Tempe and Phoenix and Palm Springs every March to watch the boys limber up and bat around, but this trip was out of Minneapolis. We were working on our fourth or fifth gin and tonic, not to mention a little Thai, and the sun was setting somewhere but we couldn't say why.

The 1981 season was looking good for the M's. New seasons always do, but the Mariners had reasons for fresh hope. That onetime great shortstop and base-stealer, Maury Wills, had been hired on as manager in place of poor old Darrel Johnson, who had become a coach at Texas. Wills, only forty-three, promised to inspire this young team and teach the guys how to run the base paths and play a bolder game, scratch and claw and win!

Grown men with too much painful experience of losing and too much baseball savvy to believe in miracles nonetheless fall prey to this kind of wishful thinking when it's March and the sun's coming on. Over the winter, the Mariners were finally sold to a rich entrepreneur, one George Argyros; the team had been owned by a consortium of six, which left six different opinions about what to do so very little got done. Attendance had been slumping down to a pathetic level, losses were staggering, and some said the team was close to banko. The team finished dead last in the major leagues in 1980, and people simply wouldn't pay to watch them stumble around in an unpleasantly plastic environment like the Kingdome. Management further alienated the fans by raising ticket prices while the product deteriorated, and removing the good, cheap bleacher seats from the ground level to the high, high upper reaches of the third-deck right-field corner, so high you could almost get nosebleed from the altitude, plus you couldn't see the right fielder at all. No team, no not even the Chicago Cubs, was more miserable in its lack of spirit, fans, glory.

But George Argyros promised to change all that. A wealthy Southern California real estate tycoon, he had the bucks necessary to pick up a few good sluggers, which he promptly did in acquiring Richie Zisk from Texas and Jeff Burroughs from Atlanta. (Zisk did handsomely, and was eventually named *The Sporting News* Comeback Player of the Year in the AL, but Burroughs was disappointing and was sent packing.) The pitching, traditionally the M's most woeful ineptitude, looked as bad as ever, but at least the hitting would be improved. (And it was. Tom Paciorek surprised everyone but the closest Mariners watchers by contending for the batting crown all season, and on the whole the team hit better. Now, if they only had pitchers. . . .)

Opening Day was as exciting as ever. Martha and I sat in the Mecca Café on Queen Anne Avenue nursing our drinks and trying to get as loaded as possible before entering the stultifying atmosphere of the Dome. The Mecca is a real person's bar in Seattle, a place for fishermen and bag ladies and street people. A square deal: cheap drink, and plenty of it. It's a remaining piece of the old Seattle I loved, now rapidly disappearing in favor of the aerospace plastic mode of living.

My latest proposal to Bowie Kuhn about how to deal with the home run surplus in the Kingdome went unheeded. The Dome, you see, allows the cheapest home run in the history of baseball. More home runs are hit there than in any other ball park, home runs that would certainly be fly balls in other stadia. The left foul line is supposed to be 310 feet but Seattle reporter J Michael Kenyon measured it at 295 feet; plus which there's no *air* in there, no wind or anything to stop the ball from flying "out," which means anything over the short fence. Since all this is true, it's not quite fair for a Kingdome home run to count as much as a real one. To correct this, I proposed a new statistical category in baseball records, that of the Dome Run, or "domer," the DR. Runs batted in with domers would be DRBI's. A ridiculous suggestion, of course, but so is the ball park.

The sweet tones of Dapper Dave Niehaus and Ken Wilson came happily through the radio of my '67 Chrysler as we tooled up and down the hills, over Skid Row, and down to the waterfront. What with Dave and Ken's announcing and J Michael's outrageous coverage in the *Post-Intelligencer*, it was hardly worth being at the games in person. J Michael often quoted Shakespeare, and one time wrote an entire dispatch without once mentioning the final score of the game.

Not that it mattered to many. Opening Day was a lot of fun, with new owner Argyros there to lead cheers, and a respectable 20,000-plus people in the hall. So what if the team lost? Nobody expected much, and it was a close game, we got our money's worth. Hopes ran high.

It didn't take long for the bubble to burst, though. Once again the new season seemed doomed by May. Maury Wills, the onetime great base-stealer, proved to be less than a terrific manager. Peter Gammons in *The Sporting News* A.L. Beat for May 30: "Wills began his regime with a faux pas in his second game, going to the mound twice in one inning, not knowing the rule. He said last winter that Steve Stroughter was being invited to spring training (he'd been traded two weeks earlier). Later, Wills said Leon Roberts was in his center field picture (he'd been traded two months earlier). He punished Rob Dressler for kicking a helmet (Rick Auerbach had done the kicking), left a spring training game early, missed most of a workout while taking a friend to the airport, taught his players to run down opposing runners to the advancing base and tried cheating by expanding the batter's box. He was telling infielder Dave Edler he was being sent to Spokane, then changed his mind when he saw Brad Gulden walk by. He tried a 1:30 A.M. bedcheck before a 1:00 P.M. doubleheader and posted a set of eighteen rules, including 'no dogs in the stadium.' "

Wills' most serious crime was the deliberate lengthening of the batter's box by a foot, a gross mistake that was discovered before the April 25 game against the Oakland A's. Maury didn't even apologize. Said Argyros: "We won't tolerate anything that isn't first class." Wills was sacked.

On May 7, Rene Lachemann came up from Spokane to manage the team, which had been losing badly. Press reports later claimed that the Mariners had been purposely losing because winning would have kept Mad Maury aboard. Under Lachemann, the team enjoyed spectacular improvement, playing nearly .500 ball and drawing about 17 percent better attendance until the end came on June 12.

29

When [impossibly skinny pitcher] Kent Tekulve
was born, the doctor slapped his mother.
—Unidentified press-box writer,
Portland, Oregon

They tore down the shack in late April and, homeless
again, I took to camping in Michael's apartment in
Portland, Oregon, which had a picture-window view of
the Mount St. Helen's volcano and a cable color TV
offering every Cubs, Mets, and Braves game and assorted network and Mariner telecasts.

We always call Portland "Poland," and the people
there "Polish." Portland is the true spiritual home of all
the Po people you ever met.

Because of the unique Oregon law that makes every
aluminum can and every beverage bottle worth at *least* a
nickel each, the Po can make a living picking up richer
peoples' discarded deposit containers and you see people
hauling around bagfuls or rolling "borrowed" supermar-
ket carts through the alleys and streets, prowling for
Coca-Cola cans.

There must be more second-hand thrift shops per
capita in Poland than in any other American city. You
can still buy a pair of shoes for fifty cents. The city is rich

in ninety-nine-cent movie theaters and free public concerts and theater, excellent used bookstores, cheap
buses. The major downtown streets are closed to traffic
other than public transit, and cobblestoned into pleasant
malls. It's against the law to drive your car into an
intersection until you are cleared ahead to get entirely
through it. You can get arrested for jaywalking, so few
do. Liquor sales are monopolized by the state of Oregon,
whose liquor stores are small, hard to find, usually
closed at 7:00 P.M., and not open on Sundays or holidays—with the second-highest prices in the nation. The
Po make do with beer.

I love the easy, can-do attitude of Oregon and the
Polish republic. It ain't fancy, but it's comfortable. They
let you live there, barely. It rains every day, too, and
when the volcano erupts there's so much ashy crap in the
air you can't breathe and have to wear a face mask.
Anybody willing to put up with these disadvantages is
welcome to be publicly spaced out in Poland.

Michael's place was a few blocks' walk from the Portland Municipal Stadium, where the minor league Beavers play in the Pacific Coast League; and, despite the
small-change nature of such a Triple-A operation, the
park and team are both splendid, old-fashioned, and
hugely enjoyable. The old wooden park's outfield walls
are covered with wonderfully hokey local billboards and
there's a dinky wood-slat press box beside the bleachers.
The Beavers, a Pittsburgh farm club, has old-time favorite players like Willie Horton and Luis Tiant, as well as a
roster of promising youngsters. Best of all they stage
crazy promotions and giveaways calculated to give a
good show even in a drizzle.

We went down there one night when some radio
station in town was doing a promo buzz. With a coupon

117

from local merchants, you could get two tickets in the grandstand for something like eighty-eight cents. Inside, the pitcher's mound was covered by a big plastic swimming pool full of cold water, three feet deep and perhaps twenty feet in diameter, topped by a diving board extending from a ladder. Under it, the entire infield was covered with the tarp they use against rain. The fast-talking radio DJ, accompanied by two slinky blondes, got on stage before thirty thousand fans and explained the rules of the game:

That is, the game before the game. Twenty lucky fans were to have their numbers called out from a random drawing of ticket stubs. If your number was called, you'd have the option of diving or plunging into the swimming pool, the bottom of which was covered with coins wrapped in gold-foil paper.

Two of those gold-foil coins were silver doubloons, valued at about two hundred dollars. *One* gold-foil coin was a *gold* doubloon, valued at *One Thousand Dollars* folks! Seventeen of those twenty coins were Susan B. Anthony dollars, Suebucks—than which most people would rather have any other currency. Suebucks are more trouble than they're worth; they're easily mistaken for quarters, and make you feel that's what your dollar is worth. They're supposed to honor women but actually demean them. The Mecca Café back home in Seattle has a sign saying they refuse to accept them. Diving into that pool on a fifty-five-degree night in Poland for a lousy Suebuck would be downright stupid, and some of the lucky winners whose names were drawn declined the privilege. Reviewing the odds, 3 out of 20 for something other than Suebucks, they accepted bribes of eight dollars each from the crazed DJ, and gave the dive to the next lucky fan.

The process of selection took a good thirty minutes, but finally twenty lucky volunteers were lined up at the foot of the ladder to the tall diving board. Some high school band played and a talentless actor in a cartoony Portland Beaver suit cavorted for the kiddies. The crowd loved it.

The men and boys took off their shirts and shoes and socks before diving, but the biggest laughs were for the fat ladies in dresses and nylons who plunged in *derrière-en-avance*. One kid belly-flopped and the youngest contestant, just eight, was attending his first baseball game ever. When all twenty dripping-wet contestants had lined up—the baseball game had already been delayed forty-five minutes—the DJ once again went into his bribe routine. "Would you give up your coin, unopened, for eight dollars? How about eighty-eight dollars?" Some went for it. Most clung to their coin and their hope for a doubloon, only to find themselves with a despicable Suebuck. The crowd roared derisively. I ordered a third beer. The silver doubloons turned up in the fifth and thirteenth rounds, and the gold doubloon way down on the eighteenth contestant, the eight-year-old boy who was at his first baseball game. This was a great hit with the fans, and I think I even shed a tear of joy for the little tyke.

They cleaned up the pool, the tarp, the stage, etc., and finally got the ballgame under way about nine o'clock. As it happened, six months later I met some friends of the little boy's family, who said the gold doubloon was a massive fraud and worth nothing close to a thousand bucks, only a couple of hundred. What do you want in Poland?

I can't remember anything about the game.

30

On the Red Sox, you're supposed to scratch your ass, spit a lot, and make jokes about women's tits.
—Bill Lee

They had torn down the shack while the Oakland A's were tearing up the American League West. The A's set a record by winning their first eleven games in a row, and seventeen of their first eighteen. That these games were played against the Minnesota Twins, Seattle Mariners, and California Angels, all of whom did poorly in '81, escaped much notice. The rebirth in Oakland and emergence of Billy Ball was the hottest thing going in baseball. Before the departure of Charlie Finley, Oakland had been the mausoleum of baseball. It was seriously alleged that Finley counted the hot dog vendors in his attendance figures. On April 17, 1979, a night game at Oakland between the A's and the Mariners drew 653 patrons; exactly two years later, on the same date in 1981, the same teams met before 50,000-plus screaming Oakland fans.

Billy Ball is something derived from scrap-iron backyard Berkeley days in not the best neighborhood where a kid had to fight to save his butt, and Joan, Billy's Mom, taught her kids to take no guff from anybody. That Billy should be chiefly famous at fifty for punching out a marshmallow salesman in a bar is pure karma-earned fate. Let's face it, Billy lacks refined social graces. Billy's one of those little guys who can't stand big guys picking on him; he's a bad boy and he's gonna get himself in big trouble one of these days.

He's also a kind of idiot-savant. He knows one thing well, and that is how to harass and drive and manipulate baseball players to take full advantage of their opportunities and win, and win often. Don't talk to Billy after he's lost. Not unless you want to run the risk of a knuckle sandwich. The A's outfield, touted as the best in the majors, has awesome power and speed: Henderson, Murphy, and Armas. Young pitchers like Norris, Keough, McCatty, Langford. Splendid, splendid. Players with names like Shooty Babbitt, Mickey Klutts, Chicken Stanley. The A's stole home plate at times and even pulled the old hidden-ball trick. Where's the ball? You're out! Bitch bitch bitch. Billy was suspended mid-season for "bumping" an ump. His tantrums are box office boffo.

The transformation of the Oakland Coliseum from a total graveyard to the wildest scene in baseball was brutally swift and not without its ugly effects. Like Comiskey Park, the Oakland park attracts something of a rough crowd. Fights in the stands are inevitable and can be scary as hell. I'd think twice about taking a small child to a night doubleheader against the Yankees before a sellout crowd of 50,000 plus. The WBA was there when Billy first met the Yanks, his former team, and the mayhem in the outfield stands bloody near got someone killed. The progressive new ownership has done an outstanding job of reinstating first-class ball to Oakland, but when you've got Billy for a manager (and general manager and chief star player) you've got to expect a few roundhouse punches to be thrown. The day I found myself protecting a five-year-old from two Samoan giants who were destroying the row of seats behind us was my last game in Oakland.

31

Asked by Tommy Lasorda if he was tired, Fernando replied, "How could I be tired? It's only the sixth inning?"

—*L.A. Times*

The early-season heroics of Fernando Valenzuela in Los Angeles were the main attraction of '81, however, and pushed Billy Ball far into the shadows. Valenzuela was simply unbelievable: a portly Scorpio who ran off to an 8–0 record with six shutouts and an earned run average of almost nothing, and yet was supposed to be only twenty years old and just out of some dark lost-jungle tribe of Mexican Mayan Indians. "This guy is a three-hundred-year-old shaman who met Mr. O'Malley (late owner of the Dodgers) in Heaven, and Mr. O'Malley said, 'Fernando, the Dodgers are in trouble,' so he came down here from Heaven to help the Dodgers out," said manager Tom Lasorda. A shaman? Where did Tommy learn that word, from Carlos Castenada?

Valenzuela's eyeballs turn to the heavens just as he releases his pitch. He doesn't have exceptional speed or control, but he mystifies batters with a wide variety of pitches, and has all the poise of a seasoned magician.

Thanks to Fernando, the Dodgers' radio audience has spread to hundreds of millions in Latin America who get Spanish broadcasts from Jaime Jarrin.

People say Fernando reminds them of Babe Ruth. He has the same round enormity, *joie de vivre*, and easy affiliation with people. He is already a legend in his twenty-first year, and whether or not he "survives" in the future, he gave us the most exciting rookie pitcher of the age. Even confirmed Dodger-haters had to love the chubby, ageless left-hander from Sonora.

In Montreal, an equally outstanding rookie, Tim Raines, was overshadowed by Valenzuela's prodigious reputation and drawing capacity. Raines simply stole fifty of fifty-five attempted bases in the first two months of the season, and but for the strike would have easily smashed the all-time stolen base record. Even watching him at close range at the ball park, he seemed a blur on the base paths, would steal second as if it belonged to him, and if the pitcher wasn't careful would brazenly take third while his back was turned. Tim could hit .300 and play left field like a gazelle and in fact may have set new standards before you read this. When the Expos, late in the season and in a tight pennant race, lost Tim to a broken hand, the fans posted a banner that read "Talent and brains and pray for Raines." He came back and played brilliantly in Montreal's doomed effort to take the Dodgers in the playoffs.

Len Barker, a heretofore unsung pitcher for the Cleveland Indians, hurled a Perfect Game early in 1981. Some said it was a fluke, but Barker's been improving. Perfect Games always take a large share of luck, anyway: one error by a teammate and your Perfection is gone. Barker's gem on May 15 was the first such feat since Catfish Hunter of the A's did it to the Twins back in 1968. Barker's opponents were the hapless Toronto Blue Jays, a bad team that had nonetheless never before gone hitless in a game.

These were just a few of the highlights of what started out to be a great season. On June 12, when the players' strike began, the standings in three of the four divisions were very close. The Dodgers led the Reds by a mere half-game, the Phillies clung to a small advantage over the Cards and Expos, and the Yankees were closely followed by the Brewers, Orioles, Red Sox, and Tigers. The Oakland A's were miles ahead of the others in the AL West, Valenzuela and Raines threatened to break every pitching and speed record in the books, and the San Diego Chicken was finally released by the courts. His rebirth, emerging from a giant egg at Jack Murphy Stadium in San Diego, had been telecast nationally the previous year. Ted Giannoupolos, who runs around doing great mime and dancing in a big chicken suit, had been declared the one and only genuine Chicken and not only stole the show at every game but prompted an army of uninspired imitations.

The season drove me back on the road again, stopping in Atlanta to feel the numb grief of the child murder epidemic, wondering how St. Louis can be so damn hot and where the hell *is* Arlington, Texas, and winding up in New York, on the piers, in the bars, or holed up in the apartment waiting for the end.

32

The Ball once struck off,
Away flies the Boy
To the next destin'd Post
And then Home with Joy.

—Anonymous, 1787

My mother's side of the family came down to New England from Trois-Rivières, Quebec, Canada, to find work in the mills of Lawrence and Lowell, Massachusetts, and Lewiston, Maine. There was always a great deal of French spoken in our home, as the older relatives spoke no English. I heard my grandmother's stories of Quebec as old-country lore, and felt a deep cultural and genetic attachment to French Canada from the first times I visited there as an adolescent.

That background may go a ways toward explaining why I'm now a full-fledged Montreal Expo fan, but it was the Montreal team and not the French culture that brought me to one of my current "home" teams, a full three thousand miles away from where I live, and in a foreign country where the winters are so severe that your tongue can freeze to your lips. I wouldn't visit Montreal past Labor Day or before Memorial Day, but when summer is in bloom I love to go back to that city and drink my *café au lait,* eat croissants, stroll the gardens and museums, haggle with the merchants in my best *patois,* taste the nightlife on Rue Ste. Catherine. Montreal is a smell of danger, a little glitter, superimposed over a European city full of cooking and day labor. When they get drunk in the streets of Montreal, which they do after every major sports victory, the party is life-threatening fun.

Don't ever let on in Montreal that you're American and don't speak French. You're immediately up against great rudeness. The political battle for independence has left pockets of very anti-Anglo feeling, and even when I can't really understand what someone's telling me, I pretend that I do. It works tolerably well, as in Japan or any other foreign country, that the things you really need to know (like "toilet" or "hotel") are plainly marked, and the most important phrases in any language are still "please" and "thank you."

The best "feeling" for Montreal I've ever seen on film is a picture called *Montreal Main,* directed by Allan Moyle, which occasionally plays at art theaters or international film festivals. Taut suspense is interwoven through the lives of very real and absorbing characters, in a kind of bilingual world that has equal parts grace and degeneration.

The Expos play at the Stade Olympique, reachable by a modern, clean subway that hums along almost noiselessly and doesn't leave you feeling like you need a shower or a gun. The stadium is a bowl or dome-type affair open to the elements at the top, where a large oval aperture leaves the pitcher on the mound "feeling like he's at the bottom of a giant toilet bowl," according to

127

Bill Lee. The oval design was supposed to prevent the rain from falling directly on the stands, but when a puff of wind comes with it, the wet stuff flies everywhere inside the park with gusto. It's a cold place, and a ball park constructed at outlandish expense to the taxpayers (over $150 million), but Montreal sports fans are rabid and loyal and obviously delighted with the complex.

As am I. My idea of an exciting time is being in the Olympic Stadium while the Expos take on the Phillies for the pennant, Steve Rogers against Carlton. In the 1979 season, Montreal finished second after taking the pennant race down to the last day of the season; again, in 1980, it went to the wire and finished a little closer second; in 1981, with the split-season nonsense, the team won its division but lost the pennant playoff to the Dodgers in the final inning of the final game. It would seem, even to a casual observer, that the Expos are doing a little better every year and are definite contenders for some World Series of the near future, a World Series very likely to be played in frigid weather with a distinct chance of snow. Whatever, the stands will be packed with fans who really believe, for whom their team stands first in their hearts. The fans can be very noisy, but their demonstrations rise and fall like waves. At times, the entire ball park falls into a hush. Then Gary Carter stings a perfect double to right-center, and the whistles and noisemakers go wild.

Even the August I spent there, nights were cold and bad weather canceled several of the games between the Expos and the San Francisco Giants I had come to see. When a night game was postponed for several hours due to rain, the Expo management opened a full bar for the writers. Bloody decent of them, I thought, to stock the best Russian vodka and Scotch whiskey. The game resumed after 11:00 P.M., with the Giants sending in Greg Minton to replace starting pitcher Ed Whitson, who'd held the Expos to one hit over four-plus innings. Minton then gave them only a hit over the second half of the game, and the Giants won it, 1–0, at one o'clock in the morning with several thousand diehard fans still in attendance, wet, cold, and disappointed. They'd be back tomorrow, or the next day.

33

It ain't over 'til it's over.

—Casey Stengel

June in New York, and there's no baseball. It's scarcely believable. The awesome reality struck me in bed, when I realized I didn't have to turn on the radio or TV or read the box scores in the *Times;* in fact, I didn't have to get out of bed. A rabid Cleveland Indians fan living in Las Vegas went on a hunger strike until the game came back. I simply lost whatever appetite I had in the first place.

The end came on the first Sunday without ball. The day was intolerably hot, and the apartment was out of everything necessary to life: no money, cigarettes, food, coffee, liquor, dope, or baseball. There was plenty of cat food, though. The owner of the apartment had trucked four cases of Buffet Brand up five flights of stairs for the comfort and nutrition of his yowling Siamese, the ultimate neurotic New York cat, while he was out of town. Meanwhile I was eating up everything in the cupboards and desperately hanging on to two phone lines and the shards of literary business.

Well, I'd read somewhere that very poor people in New York *do* eat cat food. How bad could it be? The prospect was nauseating, the more so because I loathed the cat but loved its owner, my old friend John, and so was obliged to pamper the wretched creature in the style to which it was accustomed. In the heavy humidity, it was forbidden to open the bottom parts of the windows since Kitty would then go out on the sill and perhaps plunge to her death. Can you imagine a cat that can't perfectly cling to so broad a shelf as a windowsill? Kitty *had* once plunged the five stories down the gloomy air shaft, and had survived. "It just turned into a three-hundred-dollar veterinarian bill," John said shyly. John's friends in New York tried every ploy to convince me to kill the cat while he was gone, but I didn't have the heart.

I poured myself a tall glass of poisoned water from the tap and stood at the big windows overlooking Christopher and Bleecker, trying to catch a breeze and see what was up. A marching band set up on the corner and hordes of strollers coursed down Christopher, an unending parade of the conventional and bizarre people abreast in twos. The loose-joint guys were busy as usual outside the Boots and Saddles—joint for a buck, smokable with luck. You have to actually stand there and smoke the joint in front of the guy to be sure you're not getting burned. The street trade was out early—love for sale. Blaring bad disco music poured from the bars. A few months earlier, some homophobic maniac with a Cadillac and a machine gun shot up the Boots and Saddles for no more reason than a fervent desire to rid the earth of a few of its multitude of homosexuals. He succeeded, but the scare had worn off and the place was full again. The Village Cigar store on Sheridan Square still had a plaque embedded in the sidewalk at its entrance identifying the spot as "Property of the Hess Estate, which has never been dedicated to public purposes."

Surveying the zoo below, then turning to the blank TV screen almost in crying disbelief, then turning back to the window, I spent the entire day in the apartment since I couldn't go out on the streets without a dime, there is no public comfort in the marketplace, and nothing is free. I needed a friend, and have plenty of them in New York, but every one I called was out for the weekend. Of course. Everybody who could afford to get out of town did. Those remaining who could afford air-conditioning turned it up, and others walked to the parks and riverbanks. I was too weak to walk, and anyway it seems to cost a buck a block just to walk around in N.Y.C. I resolved to lie down and die.

Day passed into night with elegant slowness. The longest day of the year was nearing us, and the sun took its sweet time setting. I took a shower and was grateful for the cool. The phone rang.

It was Spencer Holst, the sixtyish, pixieish author of *The Language of Cats*, saying he had a present for me and should he bring it over right away? Yahoo! I realized I couldn't ask Spencer for money, so no eats were in sight, but I was grateful for whatever. And surely some food-oriented friends would start arriving at their nearby apartments by midnight.

I first saw Spencer Holst in one of those step-down-a-level theaters, formerly a basement, off Third Avenue in midtown, a neighborhood of small groceries and bars. The December night was bitter and we were glad to sit on torn upholstery in the steamy room. Finally a gnomish man in late middle age, wearing what I call a Perry

Como sweater and appearing for all the world like some kind of elfin librarian, sat down on the one stool on the dark stage and said:

"Once upon a time a millionaire playboy burned his face off in an automobile accident."

The playboy in question dons a black veil and retires to opulent seclusion in his mansion, where his faithful butler arranges entertainments, lady visitors, hashish cigarettes. Meanwhile, an out-of-work actor in Times Square decides to murder the playboy, because what could be easier than impersonating a faceless recluse? The actor succeeds, and steps into a life of luxury, only to be later murdered himself by the *next* imposter; for the actor, you see, is only the latest in a long series of imposters. "No one ever knew of this," Spencer concludes, "except the butler of course, but he never told, because he *liked his job.*"

Spencer held the audience not only attentive but trembling with pure joy for two hours. Muriel Rukeyser said *The Language of Cats* was "not just a book of wry, marvelous fables," but "a matter of ecstasy." Allen Ginsberg enthused about Spencer, calling him a "patient genius" and "old Indian aboriginal storyteller" of "triple quadruple twists and contradictions." His picaresque miniatures, bizarre and surprising, nonetheless leave you with a thinking and dreaming world of immense significance.

He told us about a girl who ended wars forever by murdering forty-two Santa Clauses in costume one Christmas season in New York; about the Mona Lisa's meeting with the Buddha; about the sweet three-year-old girl who was kidnapped by bank robbers and lived in fine Miami hotels with frilly dresses and many Cokes;

133

about the world's greatest performance of Bach's *Saint Matthew Passion* and much more. Every story was fresh and startling. I was filled with the kind of admiration only another writer could summon—admiration free of envy and spiced with the thrill of discovery. Spencer had been reading in New York clubs, on radio, in theaters and churches, since I was born. But I discovered him just as each of his fans has.

Thereafter, we became New York telephone-pals, calling each other at late hours to commiserate, talk baseball, gossip and tell stories. And when my brother sublet an apartment in Spencer's building the following summer (mid-seventies), we wound up neighbors.

I was spending a hot July in the city in frustrated attempts to raise money to support my new life on the West Coast. Every night my brother and I came back to the apartment defeated by the cruel streets and blistering weather. But every midnight, or *most* midnights, if not 2:00 or 3:00 A.M., we heard an almost imperceptible knock on the door that meant "time for astral travel." It was Spencer with his latest story in hand.

"May I come in?" he asked, peering up at me through flesh-colored glasses. Very few people are short enough to peer up at me, and fewer still so polite as to ask permission to come in when they're already in their bathrobes. We invariably rushed Spencer into the kitchen and his favorite chair.

THE GREEN GARDENIA
Green green Gardenia covered with dew, planted in a flower pot, struggling for its existence . . .
Little white marbles had been tossed in the pot to make it prettier.

And the Gardenia thought they were its bones,
and shuddered in the breeze, in horror of viewing
them, so bare, so bare.
    If the Gardenia could speak, it would shriek.
    But its soul was mute.

The Gardenia found its voice by the end of the story, of course, but I'm not going to tell you what it said. That particular story appears in *Spencer Holst Stories*, the sequel to *Cats*, which also has Spencer's only baseball story, and his longest, "The Institute for the Foul Ball." He has given a voice to the flowers, the beasts of the jungle, imaginary monsters, and human beings of exotic persuasions. In so doing, he gives a voice to all of us—our inner consciousness, baffling but more meaningful than waking reality and as subtle as dreams.

Some nights we sat until dawn, living in that wakeful world of Spencer at the round oak table, bent over his manuscripts, reading in his nasal-musical public voice. Time slipped through our fingers and disappeared altogether as we passed, painlessly, into a cloud-cloaked wilderness of the mind. When Spencer stopped reading and went home to bed, his voice continued on in my mind. The sun rose then, and another grim day began.

34

When it rains, it pours. I was in a state of mild
euphoria and hopefulness. Standing at my window, my
perch on life, I noticed the LaGuardia Airport Limousine
pulling to a stop in front of my building. Impossible. The
airport limo does *not* make stops on Christopher Street,
or anywhere else for that matter. The passengers
gawked open-mouthed at the sudden parade around
them. It was about 11:00 P.M., and the true creatures of
Christopher Street were appearing from their hiding
places. The driver of the limo jumped out and ran into
my lobby, and an instant later my doorbell buzzed.

"Hey, man, it's Jack!"

Jack? Quick now, which Jack was that?

"Jack?"

"Yeah, man, let me in, I got the limo double-parked."

It was, in fact, an old friend from Seattle, not seen in
years, now living in Jersey and hauling people to the
airport to make ends meet. They called him Saint Jack in
Seattle, where he used to sit all day in the Mecca Café

136

drinking straight bourbon and weeping for the unkindnesses of people. He went to pieces, but he was always a friend, always reaching out to love people and lend a hand.

There wasn't anything Jack couldn't do. He managed a financial empire in Florida and escaped with a stack of credit cards, all legitimate, six inches thick, which he proceeded to live on in grand fashion until the house of cards caved in and he filed bankruptcy. He drove a Triumph on three cylinders from New York to Juneau, Alaska. In the dead of winter. He could be a salesman, woodsman, tycoon, lover. He was brave, good-looking, and smart, but doomed to a kind of personal Hell. He drank all the time and talked saintly babble.

The Jack suddenly standing before me on Christopher Street was a transformed man. He hadn't had a drink in years, discovered God, and was living on some supernatural plane. Saint Jack come to his heavenly reward! His eyes beamed as he handed me a twenty-dollar bill and said,

"Hey, man, the Lord told me to bring this to you."

"But Jack, you can't afford this."

"Hey man, it's not from me, it's from the Lord!"

He laughed, and ran off to rescue the startled tourists in the limo. I watched him lurch from the curb, grinning and waving up to my window; looked at the twenty-dollar bill; started to laugh and then started to cry and then went out to Sheridan Square and ate a big meal at midnight at an outdoor table under a striped awning. Ah, Manhattan, you son of a bitch, I love you true with a few bucks in my pocket, some food in my stomach, some drugs clouding my mind, and an interesting stranger beside me at the bar.

35

I honestly feel it would be best for the country to keep baseball going.
—Franklin D. Roosevelt, 1942

Do you get the feeling that phrases like "nuclear war," "nuclear arms," "nuclear power" are getting awfully familiar? I mean, when nuclear war is a Johnny Carson joke, it's a household term. Do you lie awake at night remembering the certain grim cut of Alexander Haig's jaw and his unforgettable "I'm in control here" speech following the shooting of Reagan? Do you wonder where to turn?

Me too. There aren't any politicians around that one can get excited about, and the old leaders of the shadow government of the sixties are either not around or doing something else like baseball, or working on Wall Street, or eating. I don't eat, exactly—I never eat breakfast or lunch, and have a light dinner about seven and a heavy snack about two in the morning—but will stop at nothing to sample the highly regarded dishes of the world, and so when Jerry Rubin invited me to one of his famous salons for the beautiful people on the same day that Marie Brenner reviewed the event in *New York* magazine, I realized that you would expect no less than a full report.

Jerry, who you may recall as a famous radical of the sixties, is now a stockbroker on Wall Street. Well, not a stockbroker exactly, but he works for an investment firm down there. And he hosts a weekly salon at his fashionable upper East Side apartment where the *important* and interesting people get together for wine and a catered *table d'hôte*, and Jerry gets his name in the papers.

The time was June 1981. The temperature in New York was 95 degrees and the humidity was 100 percent. Jerry had just told me I had to wear a three-piece suit to this function. Now, the only three-piece suit I own is a heavy corduroy suit I bought for ninety-nine dollars off the boys' rack at Hink's department store in Berkeley. Clearly, I'd die of the heat if I tried to wear it to the *salon*.

But on the day of the party itself, *mirabile dictu*, it rained cats and dogs and the weather turned delightfully cool. I threw on a light raincoat over the suit, and headed on up to the million-dollar bash. Almost as an afterthought, I attached an old peace-movement lapel pin to my jacket. After all, I was going to Jerry Rubin's house. He had built his name on statements like "I don't own a suit or tie," "I live for the revolution," "Barbers will go to rehabilitation camps where they will grow their hair long," and "The world will become one big commune with free food and housing, everything shared."

My lapel pin said in screaming green letters: STOP THE WAR! MARCH ON WASHINGTON. APRIL 15, 1965. It was my original souvenir of the march, and had turned up in the bottom of an old filing cabinet at my commune in Vermont.

I couldn't find Jerry's address for a few minutes,

because I was on the wrong side of Second Avenue. For some reason I expected his apartment to be in one of the red-brick row houses, and never considered the cool, ultra-modern skyscraper right on the corner. He was on the somethingth floor and I just followed the stream of well-dressed guests. Ladies clutching purses, unblemished guys with haircuts. A receptionist asked us to sign in, and Jerry came running from the front door to tell her to make sure to get my addresses—*all* of them.

Wine and beer were served in little amounts by a single bartender and the food display, while gorgeous, didn't offer much sustenance. Carrot stalks, strawberries, little dips. As the *New York* reprints scattered throughout the cool-white apartment testified, Jerry pays out of his own pocket for these affairs, and we could hardly expect him to feed this mob, most of whom looked better-heeled than Jerry is, on a junior exec's salary.

I met a TV producer, a banker, and an actress. Everything was going along fine and if the company was kind of boring, at least the wine and strawberries were pleasant and there was no baseball to be missing. Then Jerry noticed the lapel pin.

"Look at that thing!" he said of the March on Washington button. "You can't wear a thing like that to an event like this. I ought to ask you to take it off, really."

"Are you kidding? That's an antique!" said the impeccably dressed French producer standing to my left. "It's worth at least a hundred dollars at the collector's shops."

"More!" exclaimed a lady in a satiny dress.

Jerry doesn't often blush, but he did at that moment. Somehow, the irony of it all was too much. Here's a guy who made himself famous in the antiwar movement taking umbrage at an old movement button, which was

140

meant to be nothing more than a conversation piece. Furthermore, he didn't realize that it was a thing of beauty, a piece of jewelry, a slice of history.

Changing the subject, Jerry ordered me to get him a drink. "Would you go get Jerry Rubin a drink? Just tell the bartender that it's Jerry Rubin's drink," he said. He talks about himself in the third person like that. I told the man, "The boss wants his drink," and left to attend the memorial service for William Saroyan (dreary) and have dinner with Kurt Vonnegut and Jill Krementz (wonderful, lots of laughs).

Well, Jerry is still fun and still manages to interest us enough to gossip about him, but the *salon* gets only one star from this reviewer. No drugs were offered, no hard liquor served, and the food is mostly aesthetic. Dress code enforced. Go at your own risk.

36

On Lou Gehrig: "He just went out and did his job every day."

—Bill Dickey

The first days of the baseball strike were the hardest, and even though everybody said after a while I'd get used to it, it seemed that time would never come. The players and owners were at an impasse. There would be no more baseball in 1981, nor perhaps in 1982, nor perhaps forever!

For a while, I followed the strike news closely. Every morning brought the thought that there could be a break today. Surely everybody involved would realize how dumb this strike was, how you don't tamper with a winning product, how you don't slap the fans in the face. But *oh no*. Every day the news got worse.

There seemed little point in remaining in New York. Much better to have summer vacation with my little lad back in California, on the beach and in the sun. The strike had profoundly good effects on my relationship with my kid. No longer were there baseball games to distract my attention from the stuff we do together. I read three or four books a week and saw three times as

142

many movies and rekindled an interest in classical music. Went to the beach every day and did healthy outdoors activities. Drank less, ate more, smoked less, and spent less time in front of the TV. Started to feel better about myself. Started to think this baseball strike wasn't all bad. The hell with them if they don't want to play, etc., etc.

I hope I'm not symptomatic of the evolution of the average fan through this disgraceful layoff, because if I am baseball is in big trouble. Though we love the game and will always cherish it, the strike and subsequent ersatz seasons, playoffs, and World Series left a bitter taste in our mouths, a taste of ashes.

When the season resumed in August and my son went back to his mom, I went back to the ballgames with distinctly less enthusiasm than before. Suddenly, we were faced with the unprecedented situation of a "second season," the winners of which would face the winners of the "first half" in a mini-playoff series to determine the winner of the division. Meaning: The winners of the first half were guaranteed a playoff berth and had no great motivation to play well in the second half, and in fact not one of the four first-half winners also won the second half. BUT, even if they had, that winner would have had to play a mini-playoff series against the team that finished in second place in the second half. In the end the team that finished best of all in the overall year, the Cincinnati Reds, were involved in no playoffs at all.

That's putting it all in a paragraph, but I don't want to say much more about it. With a total of 713 games canceled by the strike, the season could not have been perfect no matter what the Lords of Baseball did to patch it. But they could have carried on the season

143

where it left off with a great deal less damage than they inflicted with the bogus split-season concept and introduction of a new level of playoffs strictly for television revenues.

The fans were not fooled. Attendance was down in the second season at nineteen of the twenty-six ball parks. TV ratings for the playoffs and World Series were down by a disastrous percentage.

The "second season" was not without its moments, particular plays and games divorced in our memory from the sickening machinations of lawyers and profound display of greed in the administration of the "business." Chief among these happy memories for me was Nolan Ryan's fifth career no-hitter on September 26, against the L.A. Dodgers in the Houston Astrodome. It happened to be televised on NBC's "Game of the Week" and I watched it in a small cabin on the California coast, and it happened to follow by a day a marvelous night before, and somehow the game and day were pure magic. The season being mired in an apparently endless strike, I had retreated to my perch on the Big Sur coast, at the Carmel Institute, with my son, a parrot named Herman, five dogs, three cats, fifty-five chickens, and a million butterflies.

Ryan didn't look that strong in the early innings. He gave up three walks and ran the count high on some batters, but he prevailed and by the fifth inning, when the Dodgers still didn't have a hit, the announcers were telling us that Ryan shared the major league record for career no-hitters, four, with Sandy Koufax of the Dodgers, now a coach; if he were to complete a fifth no-hitter today, it was unlikely any currently active pitcher could challenge the record for a good many years, if ever.

Ryan got stronger and more confident as the late innings breezed by, with only one scary fly ball to the outfield, nicely chased down by Terry Puhl with a backhand catch. I screamed at my TV set in sheer joy. If the birds noticed they didn't react, except for Herman, who shrieked, "Play ball! Play ball!"

I knew I was watching a piece of history. Oh, it's only baseball history to be sure, and of no consequence in this troubled world. But to me it could have been the creation of the Mona Lisa. Ryan struck out eleven and appeared in total command in the eighth. When he sauntered to the mound in the ninth, every person in the Astrodome was on his feet, and every fan watching NBC was pacing the room. I got long-distance calls between innings from other maniacal fans watching the game in distant cities, comparing notes. Could it be true? Could we be experiencing a *real* baseball game—with something terribly important at stake, a game, a gem, a privilege we had been denied, a pleasure stripped from us and gone so long we'd forgotten the thrill of it, like people who get so deep inside themselves that they don't have sex with anybody for years and years and when they finally do have sex again it's like cannons booming and fireworks going off in the sky and you just want to bust with excitement and joy?

37

We do not trust cashiers half so much, or diplomats, or policemen, or physicians, as we trust an outfielder or shortstop.

—*The Nation*, 1920

Winter set in before the World Series did in that year, the year it died in depression. By a single game, by a single run in the ninth inning, the Montreal Expos were "excepted" from the World Series and baseball was narrowly spared the problem of staging the Fall Classic in a foreign country in a winter climate. The economic depression had set in badly at the same time. The news from Washington was simple: less for the poor, the elderly, the young, the hungry, the educators, the handicapped, the artists; more for the rich, the greedy, the military war machine.

Jobs were scarce. The auto industry was reeling and the oil companies counting on record profits from the sale of survival to people facing winter's icy blasts. The tax breaks don't help the average worker, and the inflation's not letting up, not really—no matter what they tell us we can see what's going on. Strip the land, exploit the people, the Second Coming is at hand. We won't stand for it.

146

We didn't stand for any so-called World Series between two teams neither of which even finished first in its own division. And we're not going to stand for the Second Coming or the Revolution either. What's happening to us is more like an ineluctable gravitational pull into a new age, the stakes of which couldn't be higher. We have to decide whether we'd care to survive, say, the next hundred years. Are we worth saving?

Now, we have winter again in which to ponder this kind of stuff and hope, just hope, that spring will come and find us out on the green field, kissed by the yellow sunbath and praying it won't rain.

FOUR

Looking for a Miracle

38

I took my wife to see the Giants play at Candlestick Park in San Francisco. She loved it. Along about the sixth inning, she turned to me and said, "You know, dear, I believe the Giant fans are in the *majority* here!"

—Ephraim Doner

In the spring of 1982 I moved to Hollywood in search of fame and Hollywood Ball. And nowhere was Hollywood Ball more alive than in the heart and home of David Lander, the actor who plays Squiggy on the "Laverne and Shirley" show on TV. Lander got so deeply involved with the Pittsburgh Pirates that, after he became a TV celebrity with plenty of money, he bought a minority interest in the Portland Beavers, Pittsburgh's Triple-A farm club, and outfitted his swank Hollywood Hills home with an entire room devoted to baseball. We sat and watched the Cubs play the Phillies there one June morning.

Lander sat at a big wooden desk in which the Pittsburgh skyline had been hand-carved, surrounded by trophies, framed and autographed pictures of Pirate stars, ceiling-to-floor shelves heavy with baseball books, color TV wired to every baseball cable game. At about five foot five he appeared dwarfed by all this. We talked ball at a feverish pace for hours, and even called Portland owner Dave Hersh to recommend that he pick up the Spaceman, Bill Lee, recently released by Montreal.

Lander (into the phone): "What'dya mean, the Pirates don't want Lee? Just because he's *crazy?* Hey, everybody else on the team is crazy, too. Did you tell them Lee is even *white?*" (This in reference to Pirate scout Howie Haak's widely publicized remark that Pittsburgh fans won't pay to see a mostly black team, which the Pirates is. Management promptly denounced Haak, but within two weeks the team had traded two of its black players for whites.)

Lander has many wonderful stories about Pirate players, current and former, but none more amazing than the saga of the Pirate who pitched a no-hitter while tripping on LSD.

"Impossible!" I cried. (I've had a fair share of LSD in my life, though not in recent years.) "He couldn't possibly see the plate!"

"Right," Lander replied. "He walked nine men and hit a batter! But he didn't give up a hit, and got the no-hitter anyway.

"He didn't take the acid intentionally. He'd slept through an entire day and woke up on Thursday thinking it was Wednesday, a day off. His buddy brought over this stuff called 'purple passion,' and he took it before realizing he was scheduled to pitch that afternoon in the first game of a doubleheader.

"So he goes to the park and tells them he's got a sore arm, he can't pitch. But they say he's got no choice, they don't have anybody else ready. So the park is *melting* all around him and he goes in there and just throws the ball . . . anywhere . . . he can't even see the batter! And he's walking and hitting guys, but *nobody* can hit what he's throwing. They don't know *where* it's gonna be!

"After five innings he can't take it anymore, so he says, 'Hey, I gave you five innings, take me outa there.' And they say, 'We can't take you out. You're pitching a no-hitter.' "

I wouldn't have believed this story any more than *you* just did if "Squiggy" hadn't shown me a photograph of the pitcher just after the no-hitter. He looked like a man who'd just seen God: eyes burning out of his head, wildly "lost" look, blown-out acid case.

And then there's the famous first baseman who "lives on greenies" (but doesn't play for Pittsburgh), and the "70 percent solution," that being the average percentage of ballplayers who use cocaine, according to Lander.

39

The whole history of baseball has the quality of mythology.

—Bernard Malamud

Do ball players use drugs? Is the Pope Polish? Ferguson Jenkins's 1981 cocaine bust was just the tip of the iceberg. Francisco Barrios, Chicago White Sox pitcher, was also busted for coke and went to Mexico, where he died mysteriously in 1982.

When the Spaceman, Bill Lee (late of the Expos), said he sprinkled marijuana on his breakfast cereal, baseball commissioner Bowie Kuhn fined him $250, which Lee paid to an Eskimo tribe in Alaska (his "favorite charity"). (Actually, the Spaceman paid $251, "just to fuck up their bookkeeping.") When Jenkins was caught with the coke, Kuhn suspended him from baseball before he'd even been tried by law; fortunately, the outcry from those who remembered a man's right to be held innocent until proven guilty forced Bowie to lift the suspension. And Fergie's now doing antidrug TV ads aimed at kids, the major point of which seems to be "you might get caught."

But when a Pennsylvania court convicted Dr. Patrick Mazza of Reading for illegally prescribing some three thousand amphetamine pills to members of the Philadelphia Phillies, Kuhn was silent. No Phillies player was charged in the case; even though they received the pills, it was the doctor's crime to pay for. The players engaged in a conspiracy of silence on the matter, except for pitcher Randy Lerch, who was then promptly traded to Milwaukee. Kuhn lay low, essentially "covering" the players, in the "best interests of baseball."

In other words, you can suspend a guy like Jenkins before he's had a fair trial because he's only one guy, and black. You can fine the Spaceman any day because he's the Spaceman and freely admits being a flake. But you can't suspend the entire Philadelphia Phillies over a mere three thousand illegal amphetamines!

Hollywood movie stars and baseball players are notoriously fond of cocaine. It is the drug of choice for those who can afford it. But it's bad news, boys and girls. Remember John Belushi! He played Hollywood Ball, too, and lost.

(In fairness to the Phillies, I recently met a dude named Philadelphia Lou who operates a restaurant of the same name on the island of Maui, in Hawaii, and *he* claims the Phils never received those pills even though they were prescribed in the players' names. But I don't know how much to believe a guy who calls himself Philadelphia Lou on Maui and decorates his café with life-size posters of Mike Schmidt and Pete Rose. Lou never left Philly in his heart: he calls there for the latest scores.)

40

The only real game in the world, I think, is base-ball. You've got to start from way down at the bottom, when you're six or seven years old. You can't wait until you're fifteen or sixteen. You've got to let it grow with you.

—Babe Ruth

And speaking of foreign substances, let's take a moment here to honor Gaylord Perry, Seattle's Ancient Mariner, on his three-hundredth victory. I heard inning-by-inning updates on the game from my Hollywood mansion via telephone hookup. According to *The Ultimate Baseball Book*, edited by Dan Okrent and Harris Lewine, "Perry's agent approached the makers of Vaseline, the product Perry reputedly used for his spitball, for a possible endorsement contract. A company representative replied, "We soothe babies' asses, not base-balls.'"

Perry's accomplishment, like Ryan's fifth no-hitter or Yaz's three-thousandth hit, is one of those milestones we'll seldom have the privilege of seeing again. Maybe it's because the old guys came up in the days when Vaseline, not cocaine, was the forbidden substance.

41

If somebody came up and hit .450, stole 100 bases and performed a miracle in the field every day, I'd still look you in the eye and say Willie [Mays] was better.

—Leo Durocher

"There will be an anniversary celebration in Los Angeles this year and everyone is invited to the party," the press release began. "Dodger Stadium, home of the World Champion Dodgers, celebrates its twentieth anniversary in April and like a rare fine wine she has aged beautifully through the years."

Gimme a break. There's no denying that Dodger Stadium is a beautiful facility, a great place to watch a ballgame. But I couldn't help doubting, back in the spring of 1982, that "everyone" was invited to the party—specifically not the thousands of Mexican-American people who lost their homes in Chavez Ravine when the city evicted them to clear the land for Walter O'Malley's Brooklyn Bums.

The Dodgers are the most successful franchise in modern baseball. Not in games won-and-lost, mind you, but in dollars and cents. Since the stadium opened in

1962, they've averaged 2,395,537 fans in attendance per season, and have had several 3-million-plus seasons. No other team in the major leagues has come close to that mark. In 1982, they expected to sell between 25,000 and 30,000 season tickets, which meant half the ball park would be sold out before the first game began.

And that wasn't all. Since in order to lure O'Malley to L.A. in the first place they had to promise him his own stadium—*ownership* of the stadium—the Dodgers themselves own the park outright, and need not bother, as do many other teams, with complicated leasing arrangements with the city or county government. The club also owns its own refreshments and souvenirs, parking lots, charter airplane, and showcase spring training site in Vero Beach, Florida. Every time you buy a beer or hot dog or park your car at Dodger Stadium, the revenues go directly to the organization rather than through concessionaires, as is the common practice with other teams. The Dodgers' TV and radio revenues are second only to the New York Yankees', and the club gets 20 percent of attendance revenues in other cities when the Dodgers play on the road.

The Dodgers in 1982 were still owned by the O'Malley family, presided over by Walter's son, Peter, a graduate of the Wharton School of Business at Penn. Not surprisingly, Peter was running the organization like any major corporation, not as a game, but as a serious business. The actual worth of the club was a closely guarded secret, but there was no question it was the richest operation in baseball, surpassing even the mighty Yankees.

And there's no question that Dodger Stadium is the MVP, Most Valuable Property, the team owns. It is the crown jewel in the O'Malley family tiara, the Taj Mahal of baseball.

The Dodgers stole the place. Legally, of course. Amid all the pomp and circumstance of the slick public relations campaign "celebrating" the twentieth anniversary of the stadium, the one part of the story that appeared nowhere was the fact that to build the stadium, the city destroyed an active Mexican-American community without regard for the lives of its citizens.

The ensuing bitterness of the Mexican community toward the Dodgers has become one of the clichés of baseball. Just as black people don't go to Fenway Park in Boston, Mexican people didn't go to Dodger Stadium for twenty years, until the team finally came up with Fernando Valenzuela.

When Valenzuela pitched in L.A., the Dodgers drew an average of 9,500 extra fans, all of them buying beer, hot dogs, and various bric-a-brac. All but one of his appearances there was a sellout. The TV ratings of Valenzuela's games shot to the top. He packed them into other cities, too; the New York Mets, who averaged a little more than 9,000 fans per game last season at Shea Stadium, drew 37,000 for Fernando's New York debut. He drew sellout crowds in San Francisco, Montreal, Philadelphia, Houston, Chicago, you name it. The Dodgers' one Spanish-language radio station, KTNQ in Hollywood, expanded to thirty stations in Mexico and Latin America. Fernando was invited to the White House and the home of the President of Mexico. He literally made millions of extra dollars for the Dodgers.

But when Valenzuela asked for $850,000 in 1982, the Dodgers flatly refused to negotiate. As a second-year player, Fernando was not eligible for arbitration and couldn't demand a trade. The Dodgers offered him $350,000 and didn't budge. He held out, but gave in. Meanwhile, the *L.A. Times* and the rest of the straight press actually claimed that even the Mexican community had withdrawn its support for Fernando.

The racism inherent in the anti-Fernando press was not even thinly veiled. A *Times* sports column stated that Valenzuela "should thank the Virgin of Guadalupe that he's working." Edwin Pope in the *Daily News* said, "How much market is there for Babe Ruth in Navajoa, Sonora, Mexico? . . . Wherever you are, Fernando, I bring you news from the United States. Roughly .0000000176 of America thinks you should get $800,000."

Only Frank del Olmo in the *Times* came to Fernando's defense. "[The Dodgers] are not the only top corporation in this city that has a hard time understanding the Latino community. They have been insensitive to Latinos before," he wrote. Cartoonist Bill Mauldin of the Chicago *Sun-Times* sketched a tiny Fernando crushed between two hulking monsters: a bat-wielding "Dodger Management" and a big, black umpire labeled "U.S. Immigration." The caption is, *"One* strike and yer out!"

Valenzuela returned to Sonora. It reminded me of being a little kid in Boston and hearing the grown-up men shout at Latino players who struck out: "Send 'im back to Puerto Rico!"

When Fernando at last surrendered to the Dodgers and reported to spring training in Vero Beach, he was quoted as saying, ". . . I am not a boy. I am a man, and I have the same need to be considered with dignity and respect as does every other man."

42

I bleed Dodger blue, and when I die, I'm going to the Big Dodger in the Sky.

—Tommy Lasorda

Meanwhile, back to the stadium question. Trying to get through the heavy veneer of Dodger public relations and to the truth of the matter was no easy task. The media-relations guys at the stadium were more than cordial to me, but they had nothing to say about Fernando or the Dodgers' relations with the Mexican community. Publicists Steve Brener and Steve Ross gave me access to the Dodgers' scrapbooks from 1958–1962, in which not one word about the eviction of the Mexicans was preserved. All kinds of hoopla about the building of the wonderful stadium; nothing about the displaced residents of Chavez Ravine. Where did the people of Chavez go?

I began to despair of finding them until a small miracle happened. A seventy-one-year-old novelist friend from Carmel, who spent thirty-five years in the barrios of East L.A., pulled into town on a visit and offered to help me. Within a week, he'd arranged a Sunday afternoon meeting for me with Connie S. Rios, a Chavez survivor,

161

and her family in East L.A., and Mrs. Rios in turn put me in touch with other people who'd lost their homes to the Dodgers.

The house on East Avenue 28 was pleasant and comfortable. Mrs. Rios, Bobby Verdugo, and the family made me feel at home and created a picture for me of the life in Chavez Ravine before O'Malley and the bulldozers came. The community wasn't large, perhaps 250 families, but it was a close-knit neighborhood and a good life, with unpaved sidewalks and little handmade homes.

When the city came, the people who owned property were offered the bottom-line price. "Some people sold out for five thousand dollars and some of those houses were pretty nice. They couldn't buy another house for that price, but five thousand dollars, it seemed like a lot of money."

Some families held out, and wound up with seven or eight grand. One widely publicized case involved a mother of thirteen children who refused to sell her house, and was physically evicted.

Rudy Salas lost his home, and swore that he would never enter Dodger Stadium. When, a few years ago, his sons were invited to play music there, he refused to attend.

Is Mrs. Rios bitter? "Well, you can't hold a grudge," she said. "If your memory is too long, you just make yourself miserable."

Mercedes Sandoval was a young girl when her father was forced to sell his two homes for five thousand dollars each. "My father was very upset. He put a lot into those houses. He had just finished a patio, all cemented, and fixed everything up nice. We were living comfortably, and the houses were all paid for.

"He got ten thousand dollars for both houses, but he had to go into debt to be able to buy another home. It wouldn't have been so bad if they'd offered enough money. But they told him, 'Look, all the extras you put into the house don't matter, we're only paying you for the land.'

"The streets weren't paved, and my father had chickens and goats . . . it was like a little ranch. When people came over, we could just go in the yard and kill a chicken for dinner. When they forced us out, he couldn't keep his animals. It really hurt him to get rid of his little animals.

"My father was still a young man, then. Other people of advanced age, who couldn't work, they had it a lot tougher. Most of them had their homes paid for. It was very hard.

"The Ramirez family, Seraphim Ramirez, they had a little store where we got our groceries. They couldn't afford another business after the city kicked them out. The mother got so bad they had to hospitalize her. I remember, they said, 'They can't take our property away!' but they took it.

"My mother was so sad. She cried and cried. Everybody was very unhappy. My father later had a stroke, and my mother never really recovered.

"Isn't that the way it is all the time? The rich don't care who they hurt. They just hurt and steal from the poor people, and they don't care. It's just like Ronald Reagan."

43

Idol of cheering millions
Records are yours by the sheaves.
Iron of frame they hailed you
And decked you with laurel leaves.
                    —John Kieran on Lou Gehrig

The old Dodgers, the Ebbets Field bums, were another story. Susan Litwin, writing in *Los Angeles* magazine, remembered that "all the habitués of Ebbets Field, it seemed, were old pensioners with two-day beards and burly guys with tattoos," not Hollywood-chic starlets and pretty surfer boys. The team was the first to integrate (Jackie Robinson) and had sweaty, macho heroes like Pee Wee Reese, Roy Campanella, and Van Lingle Mungo.

Van Lingle was before my time by quite a few years. His glory years with the Dodgers were the mid-thirties. He pitched a no-hitter in 1934, after which he became the namesake of a popular tune. "Van Lingle Mungo" is still heard on the airwaves from time to time, especially on J Michael Kenyon's "Sports Talk" show on KVI in Seattle. The Dodgers brought Van Lingle out of retirement at the 1980 All-Star game in L.A., where a new starlet crooned his song to him. Great fun!

I was born in 1946 and started hearing about Van Mungo as a grade-school kid. People wanted to know if I was related to him, and since there aren't too many Mungos around, I figured I was. Actually, nobody in my family is quite sure of what the relationship might be, as Van came from another branch of the clan. But I've been "carrying" the guy for thirty years, and decided to meet him.

Van Mungo, Leo Durocher wrote, "talked like Edgar Bergen doing Mortimer Snerd from the bottom of a well." He is a great raconteur who loves to tell stories of the old days, stories of dubious accuracy but great entertainment value. In Van's stories, he always emerges heroic. That the Dodgers of the mid-thirties were a lot less than heroic hardly matters. (Giants manager Bill Terry in 1934 said, "Is Brooklyn still in the league?") Van had three twenty-game victory seasons in succession, and was tagged for the loss in the second All-Star game.

I can feel the soft night air and smell the bougainvillea outside Van's retirement home in South Carolina. We sit on the porch, him in his rocking chair, me with a cigarette and a Pabst's Black Label beer (from which he steals sips, defying his doctor's orders: "If a man can't have the occasional drop, he ought to hang it up and carry me home to die"). I ask him to tell me about the no-hitter—again.

"There are no-hitters and no-hitters. Mine was the greatest one they ever saw in Brooklyn, or anywheres else. It would of been a perfect game, too, except for that umpire who called my fastball straight down the middle high and outside. He was blind. I offered to get him some glasses, and he damn near threw me out of that game. 'Listen, wise guy,' he says, 'I don't care if you

165

got a no-hitter going or not, one more crack from you and you can take an early shower.'

"But the people there, they seen it was down the pike. Not high and outside. You tell them, it was really a perfect game except for that ump. You ask Dutch Leonard, he saw it."

Is Dutch Leonard still alive? Most of these good old boys are gone now. Van's along in years, too, but he can still spit a country mile and on days when he wakes up feeling good, he's almost ready to take the mound again. In his mind, he never stepped down.

Nor in mine. Because in fact I never really met him. My letters to South Carolina go unanswered. But that summer night on the porch is as real to me as Van's memories of his greatness are to him. I've heard the tales and read the interviews. And dream the endless dream of the roar of the crowd.

44

By and large it is the sport that a foreigner is least likely to take to. You have to grow up playing it, you have to accept the lore of the bubble-gum card, and believe that if the answer to the Mays-Snider-Mantle question is found, then the universe will be a simpler and more ordered place.

—David Halberstam

Dreams don't turn to dust, but just pass on into the atmosphere and give way to new dreams-come-through. The heart savagely insists on the real thing and will not be stirred by artificial passions, small talk, or making do. The heart turns to that which sets it afire, scorching all obstacles aside. First you get a hit and then you get on base, or sometimes you can walk or even get on base on an error. In courtship, this is parallel to the first time your fingers touch, accidentally, under the table in the Italian restaurant with candles and wine; a code word in the conversation, or even a meaningful glance. You're on base. Your task is to advance, to try to come home, to *score*.

It's not that easy. You need help from your mate. You could steal if you're fast, dash to second while the pitcher is off his guard or in his motion. But you will still need another hit to get home. A sacrifice fly advances you to third, and *voilà!* you slide in at the plate! Safe by an inch! By a mile.

It's a boy's game, a game of inches. It's endless and infinite and boys' hearts swell at the thought of playing it, in the sun, in the field, on a beautiful golden day in September, for the pennant, for the championship and companionship.

Looking for miracles is a tricky business, but all of us have the same dreams: would-be miracles. We want to be rich, that is to have everything we want and need. We want to be loved and to love the others. Love is the mortar that reseals our bond, and gets us safely home. And we want one more thing, a taste of the divine, a moment in eternal bliss.

Whether it's a home run sailing out of the park, a flight to the moon, or the pounding of your lover's heart in your ears, it's great to be alive. Our love for the game is the only thing that keeps it alive, and as long as the guys love to play the game will go on.

I think there'll be spring and if there's spring we'll play ball.

RAYMOND MUNGO was born in Massachusetts in 1946 and grew up a Red Sox fan. Today, he lives in the Pacific Basin between California, the South Pacific, and Japan, and roots for the Montreal Expos. He is the author of six earlier books, including *Famous Long Ago*, *Total Loss Farm*, and *Return to Sender*, and many articles in newspapers and national magazines. The founder of Liberation News Service and former Religion Editor of *Mother Jones* magazine, he is now a director of the Writers' Baseball Association and is at work on a screenplay of *Famous Long Ago* and a novel, *Almost Grown*.